MADman From Mexico

Sergio Aragones' most indelible work was done when he was five. His parents took him visiting, to the resplendent home of a hidalgo, and left him to entertain himself in the high-vaulted sitting room of the Spanish nobleman. Mr. and Mrs. Aragones had spent a pleasant afternoon on the patio with their host and hostess when it occurred to them to call Sergio to the table for some goodies. Mrs. Aragones went to the sitting room to find that her young son had embellished the four alabaster walls, baseboards to ceiling, with crayon combat of Conquistadors and Indians. Ruefully, Sergio recalls, his father left him as worn down at the nub as one of his played-out crayons. Sergio also reflects, "Good theeng they didn't have Magic Markers in those days!"

Whatever the consequences of his early unsolicited art, Sergio's friends beg him to draw on their walls today. In the summer of 1962, this exceptionally tall, dark and handsome junior prototype of Gilbert Roland, and amalgam of El Cid and Zorro, stepped into the MAD offices. As our gaze shifted from his animated black mustache and peeled-almond white teeth, we glimpsed the artist's folio under his arm. In beguiling Inverted English, he requested that we look at some of his cartoons. Within minutes, he sold us a humorous spread on astronauts, which subsequently appeared in MAD #76, entitled "A MAD Look At The U.S. Space Effort."

It was ever thus. Cortez had a way with Montezuma!

Sergio Aragones Domenech was born in Spain, almost three decades ago. When he was six, his parents moved to Mexico City where his industrious father, Don Pascual, worked his way up in the motion picture industry; from extra, to actor, to Producer. It occurred to us to ask Serg why he hadn't taken advantage of his "proximity" to a motion picture Producer. Sergio responded candidly, "I don't think I'm such a good actor."

Continued on page 5

VIVA MAD!

By SERGIO ARAGONÉS

Edited by
ALBERT B. FELDSTEIN

With a Foreword
by Jerry De Fuccio

WARNER BOOKS

A Warner Communications Company

WARNER BOOKS EDITION

Copyright © 1968 and 1975 by Sergio Aragones and
E.C. Publications, Inc.
All rights reserved.
No part of this book may be reproduced without permission.
For information address:
E.C. Publications, Inc.
485 Madison Avenue
New York, N.Y. 10022

**Title "MAD" used by permission of its owner,
E.C. Publications, Inc.**

This Warner Books Edition is published by
arrangement with E.C. Publications, Inc.

**Warner Books, Inc.
666 Fifth Avenue
New York, N.Y. 10103**

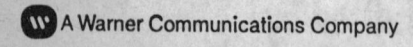

W A Warner Communications Company

Printed in the United States of America

First Printing: August, 1975

Reissued: March, 1987

10 9 8 7

ATTENTION SCHOOLS

WARNER books are available at quantity discounts with bulk purchase for educational use. For information, please write to:
SPECIAL SALES DEPARTMENT, WARNER BOOKS, 666 FIFTH AVENUE, NEW YORK, NY 10103.

We MADmen know otherwise! Serg is a fine actor and a brilliant mime. On one of our annual MAD trips, while in Puerto Rico, Serg entertained us with his underwater enactment of a home inning of baseball. While fully submerged, he represented the meat of the batting order, called all balls and strikes, acted out the disgruntled catcher, and climaxed it all by running the bases on an inside-the-pool home run.

On the same trip, a dozen of us were seated expectantly around a table in a very exclusive restaurant. Steaming platefuls of fine foods had just been served. Before any of us could turn a tine, globs of cold Russian Dressing were ladled out on our individual portions, by a swiftly moving red blur. Serg had donned a waiter's scarlet jacket, and, with undetected and affected servitude, had turned our epicurean feast into the melange you'd see on Army mess kits.

Sergio sold his first cartoon when he was sixteen and in high school. A Mexican humor mag paid him twenty pesos, $1.85. Serg kept right on drawing and selling while attending the School of Architecture at the Universidad Nacional de Mexico. His compulsion to build a better laugh won out over his desire to build a better edifice. He went into gag cartooning wholeheartedly, doing a weekly page for "Manana." He still maintains that weekly space for sentimental reasons. Serg augmented his cartooning by creating special effects for the movies and doing TV animation and advertising. He taught Mexican Popular Art, consisting of ceramic and lacquer work and silver jewelry design, to American students at the University of Mexico. One of his most apt students, blonde and willowy Lilio Chomette, was to attract him eventually to the U.S.A. and the altar. By the time Sergio came to Los Angeles in January, 1962, in quest of his Golden Fleece, he had already sold two thousand cartoons. After a brief sojourn in California with his affianced, Sergio headed in the general direction of New York City and the specific direction of MAD.

With his initial sale to MAD, he made the rounds of other prestige magazines and began to pick up checks with startling regularity. Turning west once more, Sergio married Lilio and brought her back to their adobe apartment in Manhattan. With renewed vigor, he settled down to service at his drawing-board. Since then, he has graced the MAD office and MAD pages with his cartoon themes, cover ideas, and marginals, the latter being his very popular "Drawn-Out Dramas" that keep the readers rolling in the seams, borders and aisles of MAD. When he *isn't* "thinking MAD", which is rare, Sergio does book illustrations, album covers, and is often called upon to pep up specialized booklets and guides for industry and management.

Recently, he folded his drawing board and took his own camera crew to Mexico to film an hour-long documentary on bull-fighting. He came back to the States with eight hours footage of exquisite color film, shot in various plazas and ranches and arenas throughout Mexico.

Sergio stops in at MAD almost daily, whether it be mid-afternoon or after hours; just as long as the lights are still on. He never knocks. There's no mistaking his rhythmic flamenco stamping and clapping in the hall.

He loves to fraternize with his fellow MAD artists. Sometimes you will find him alone, in the Current Art drawer, studying pen lines, textures and techniques. It's then that you know he possesses "the Cellini touch", wherein the pupil has the capacity to outshine the teacher.

Eventually, Lilio will phone and tell him to come home to supper. And, after supper, he draws.

Jerry De Fuccio
Jerry De Fuccio
Associate Editor
MAD Magazine

VIVA KARATE!

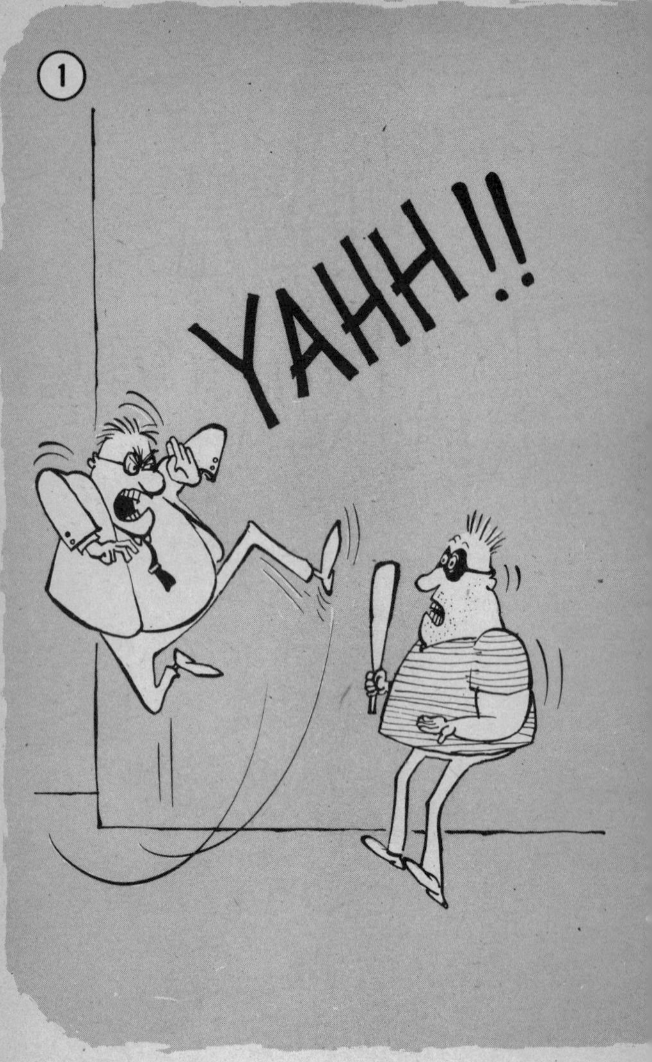
1
YAHH!!

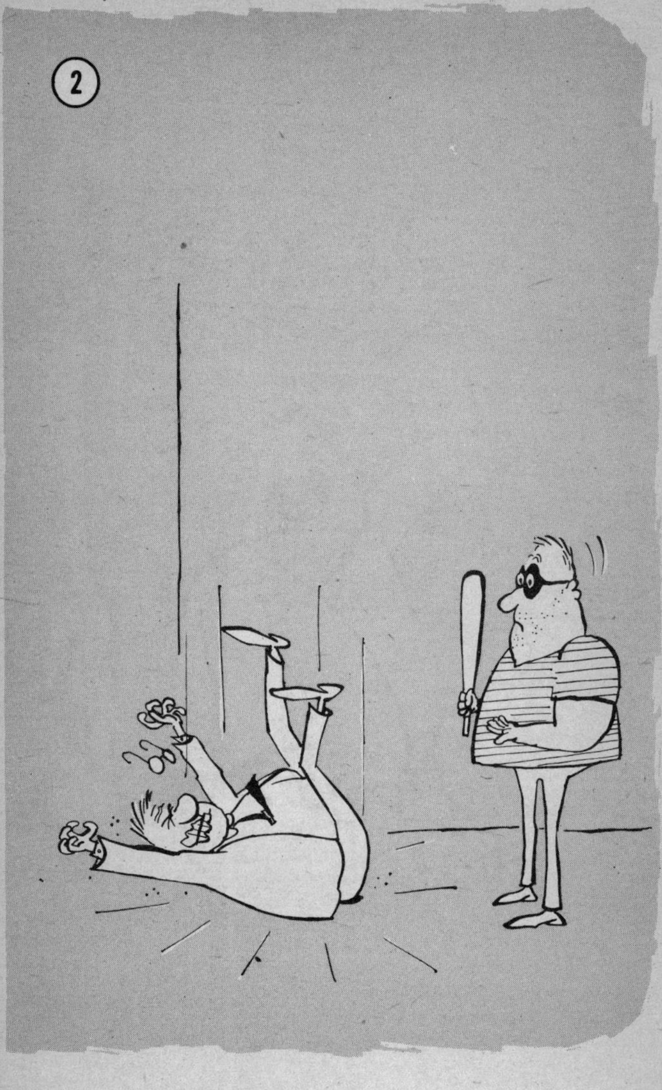
2

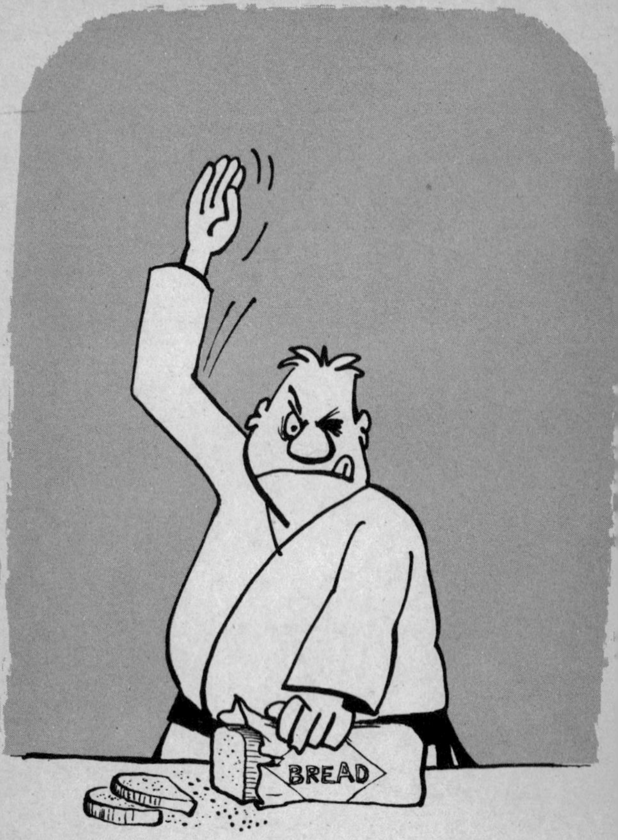
BREAD

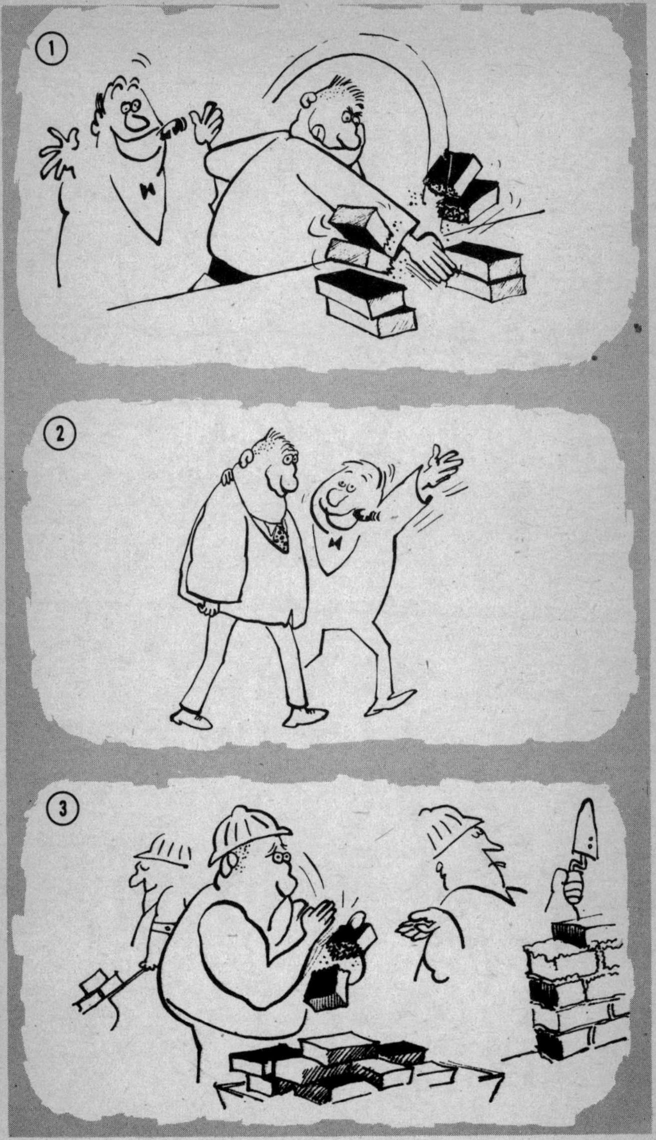
1
2
3

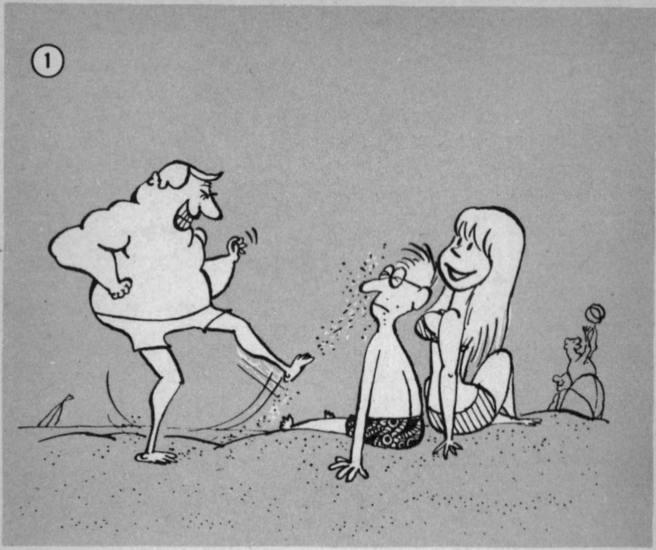
1

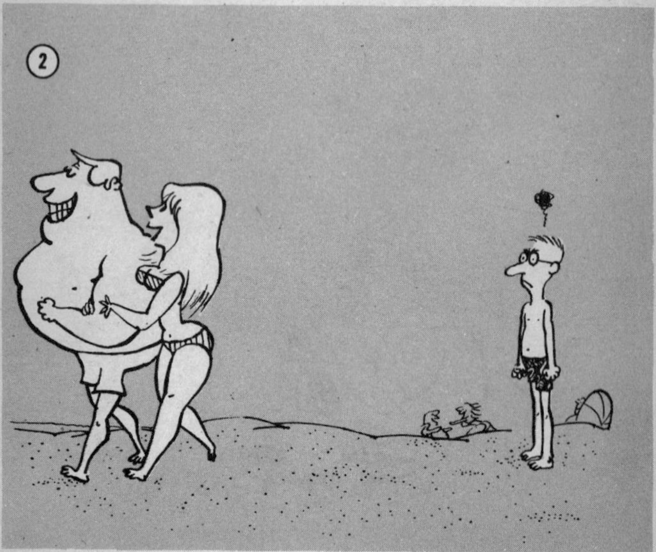
2

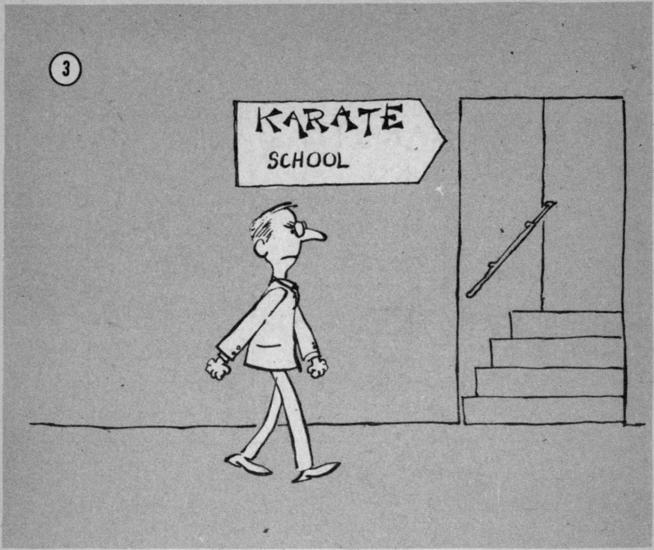
3
KARATE
SCHOOL

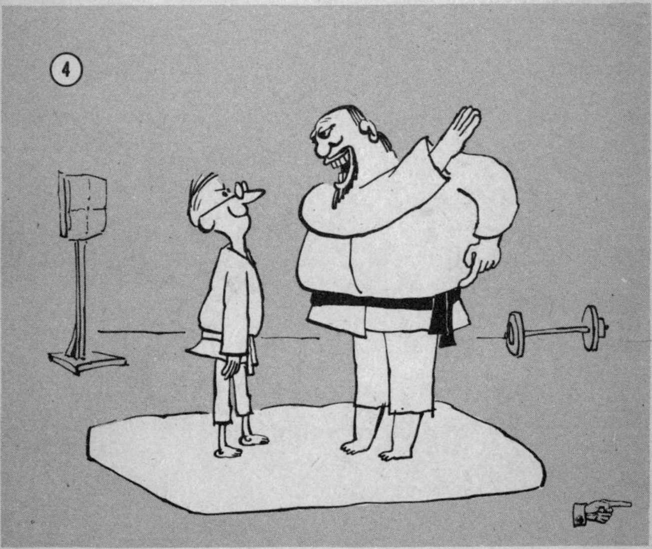
4

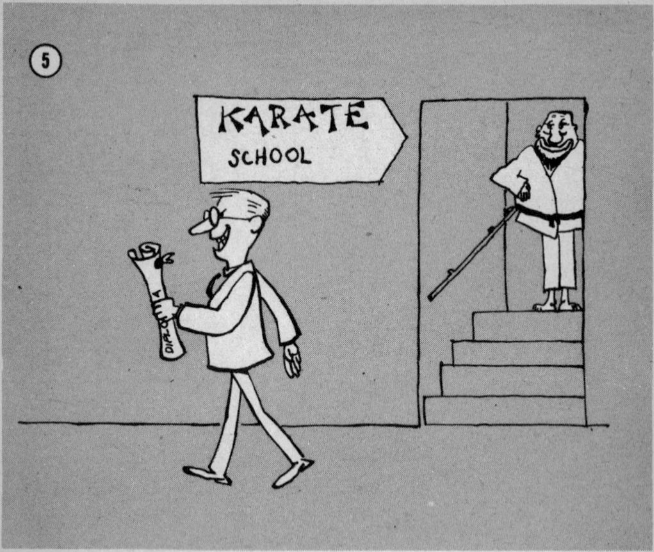
5
KARATE
SCHOOL

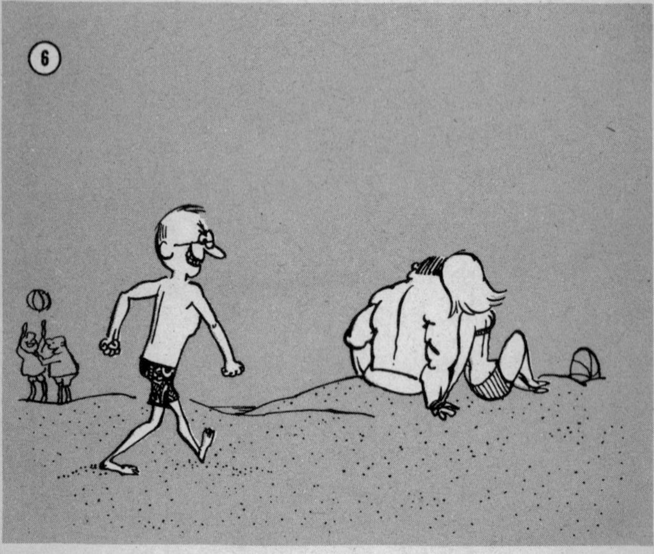
6

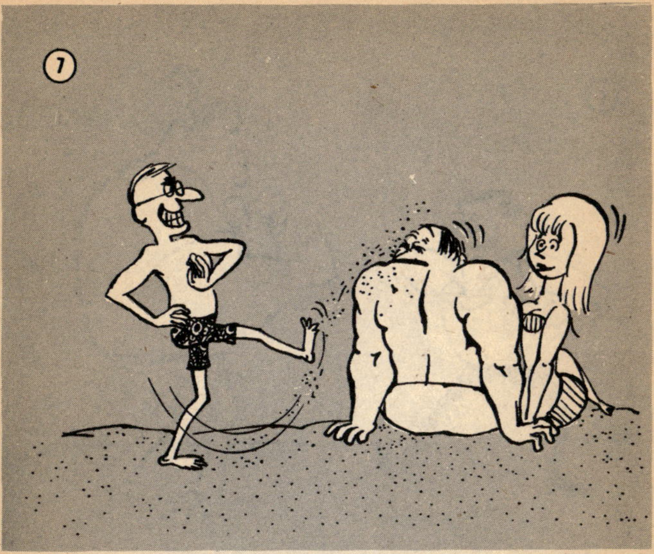
7

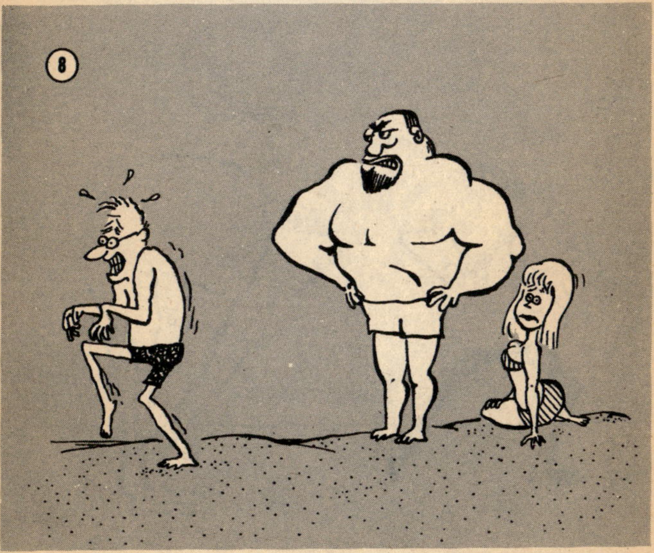
8

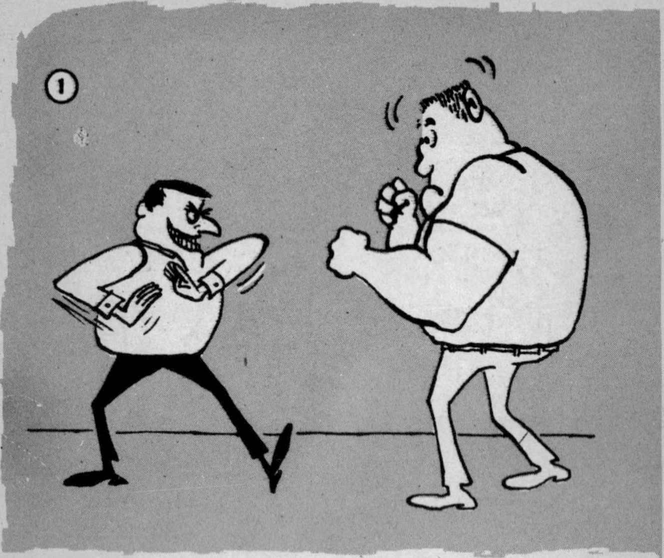
1

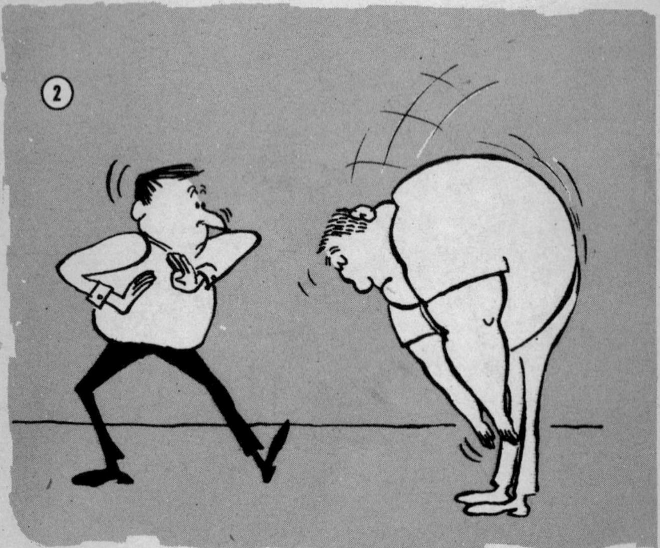
2

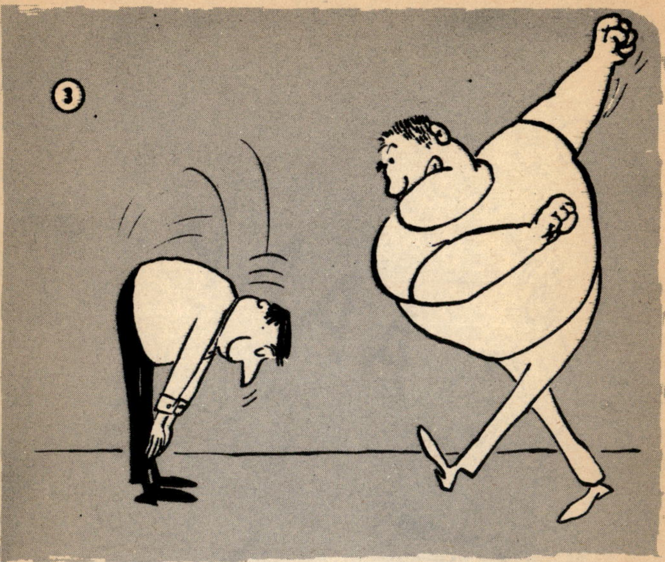

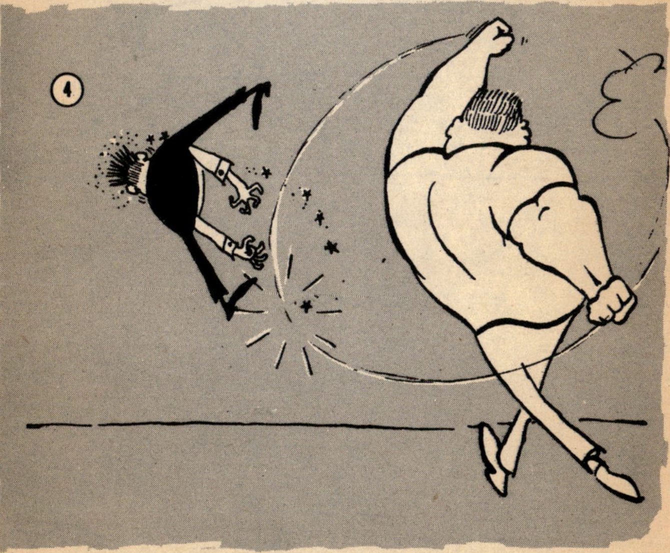

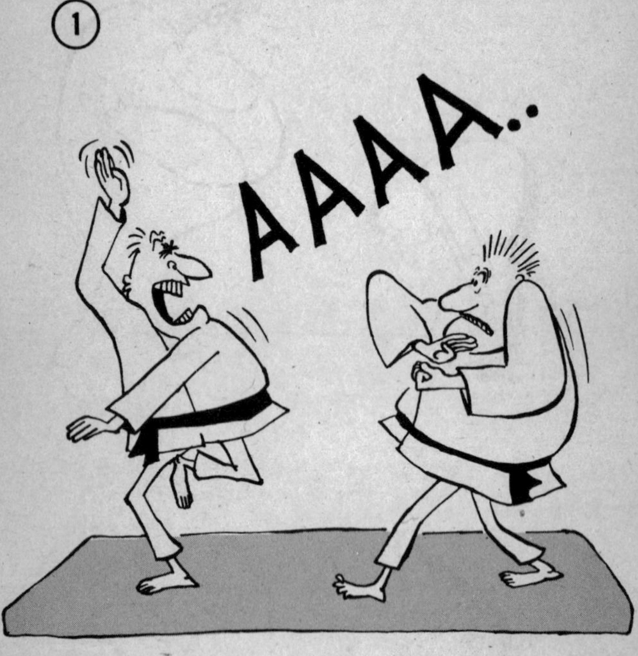
1
AAAA..

(2)

CHOOOOII!

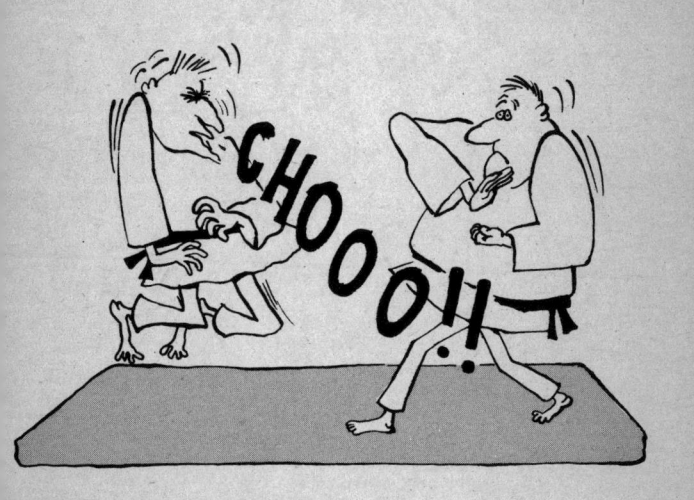

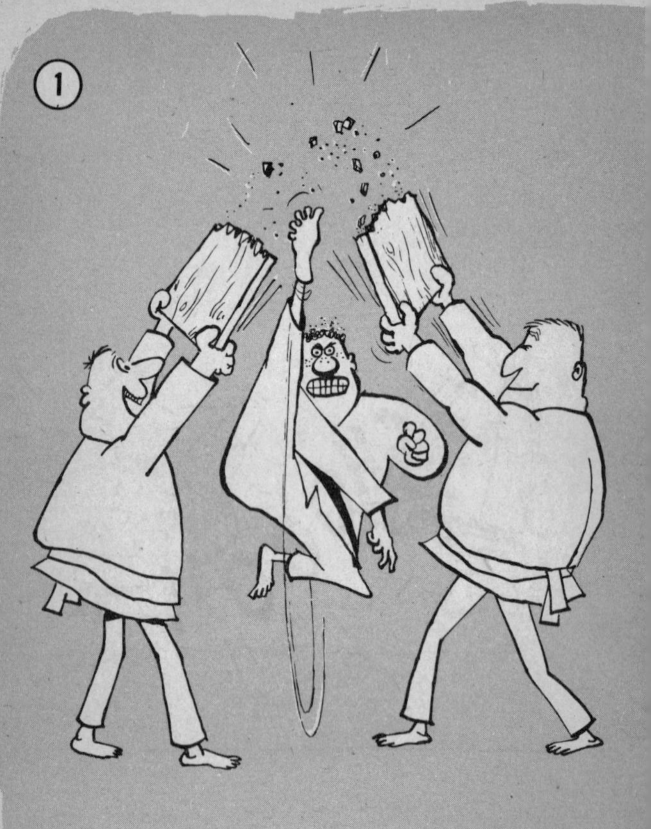
1

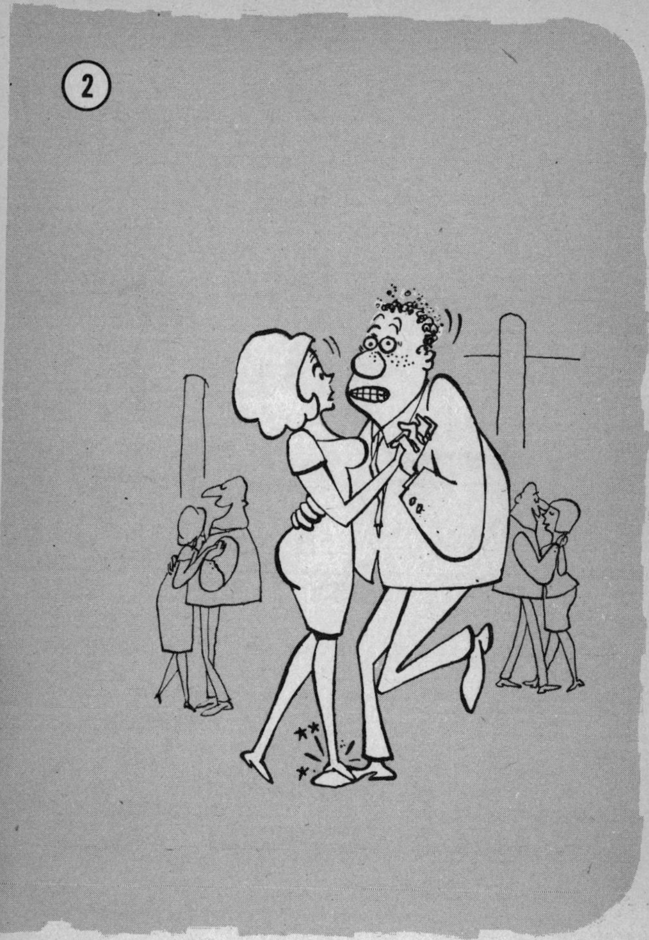
2

①

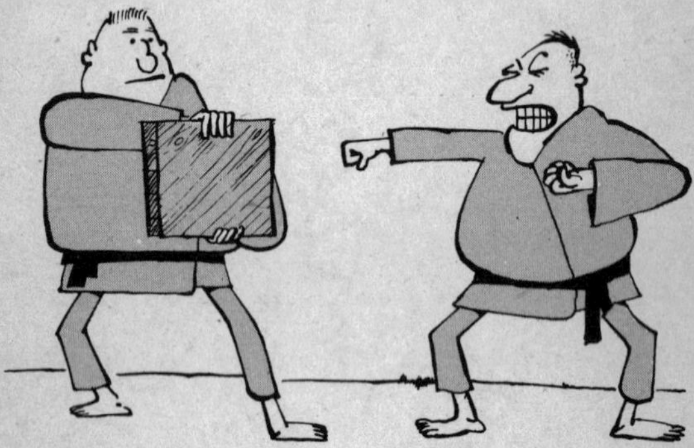

②

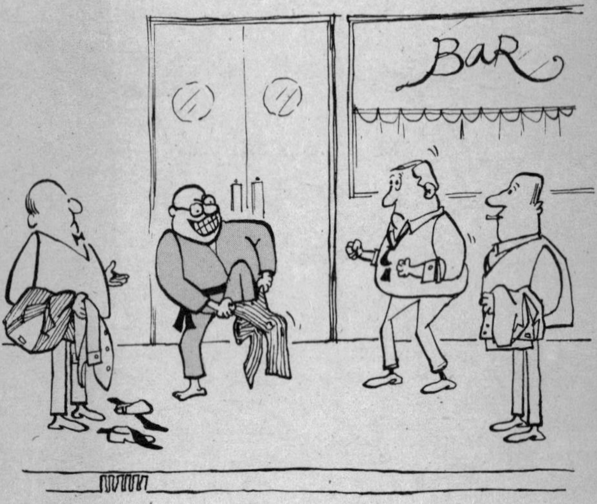
BaR

VIVA SHADOWS!

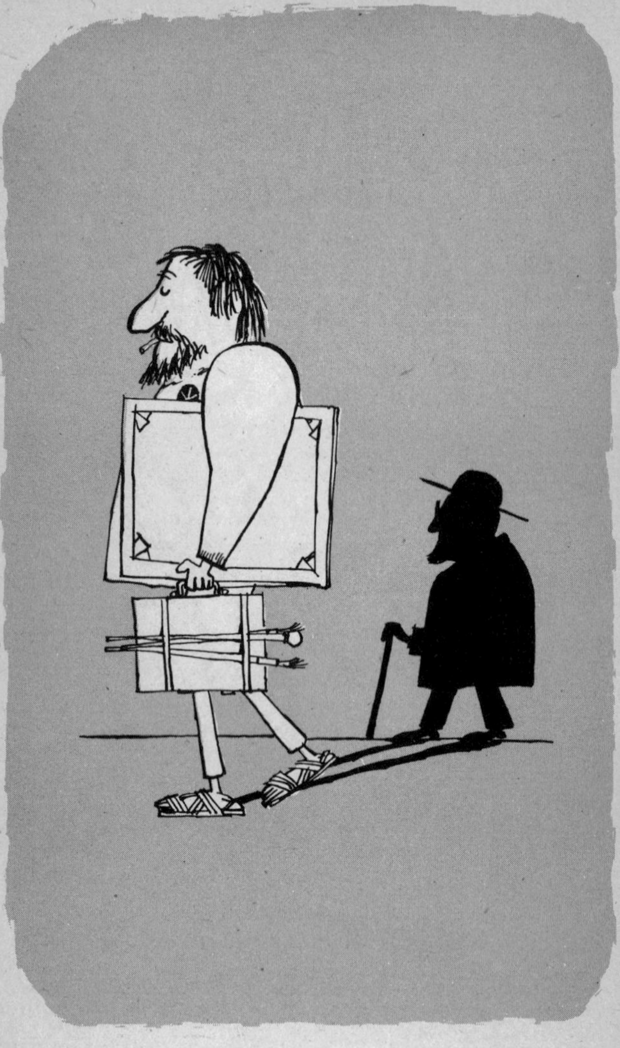

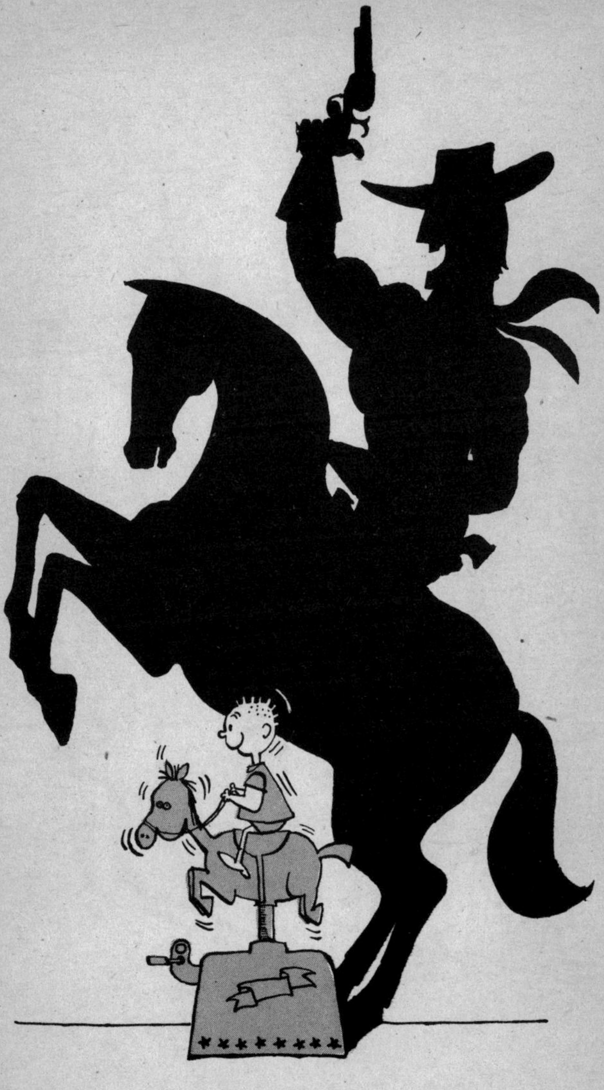

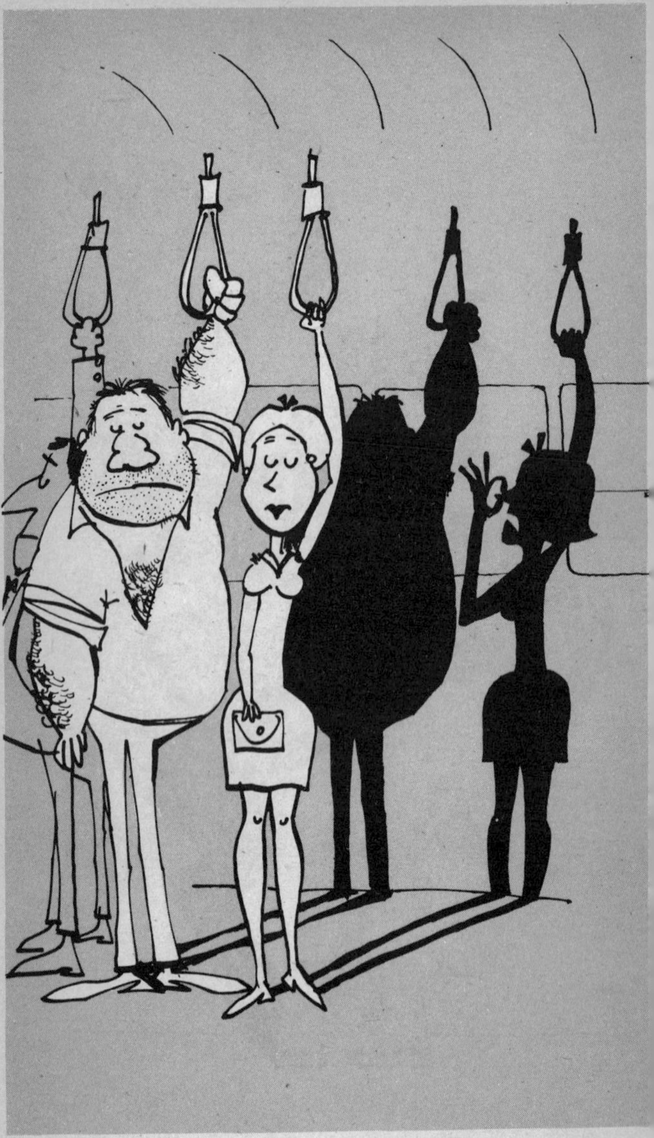

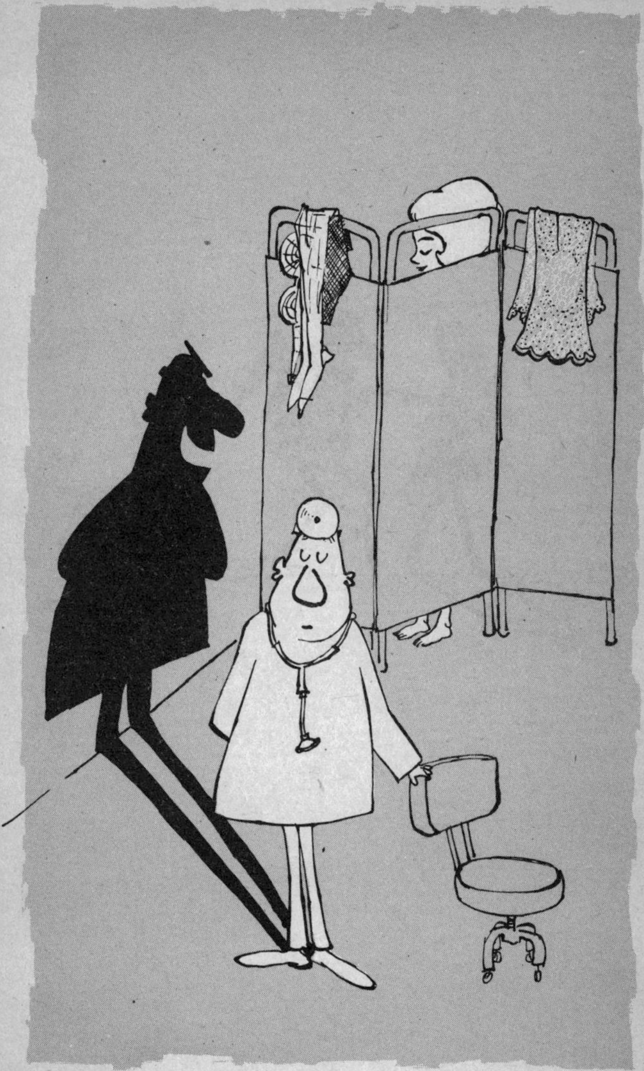

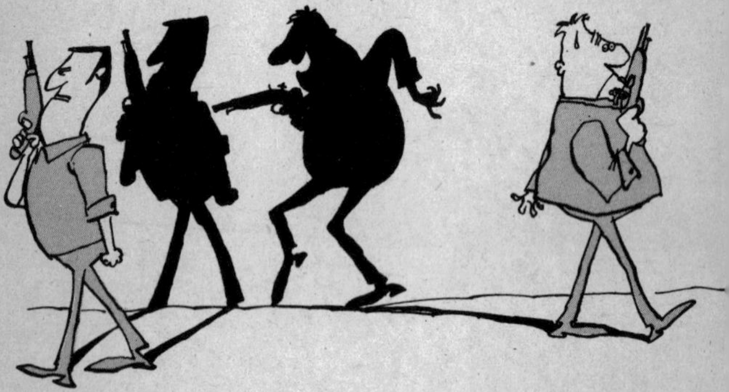

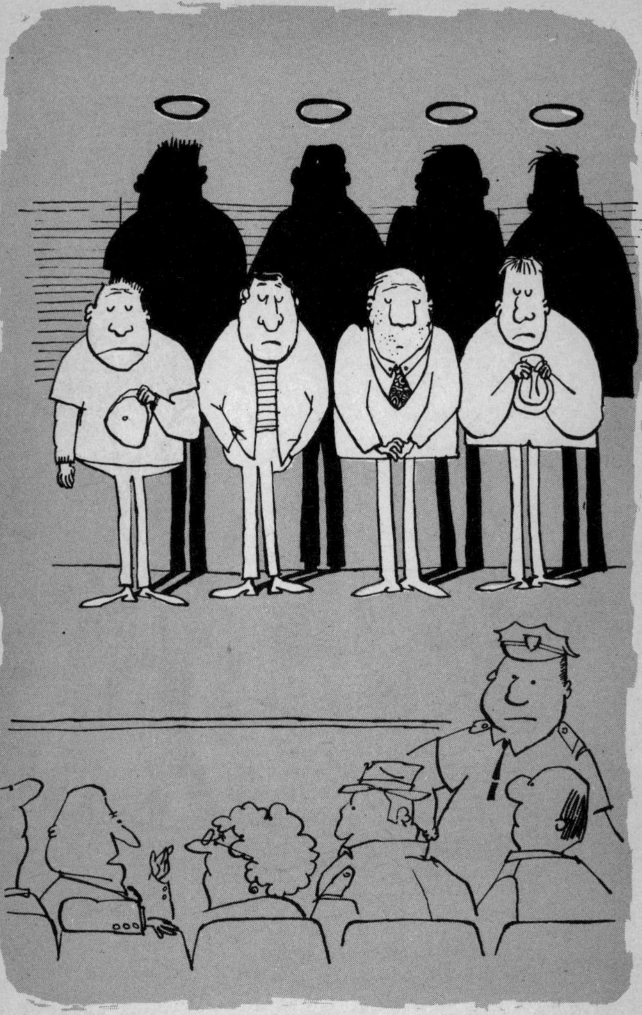

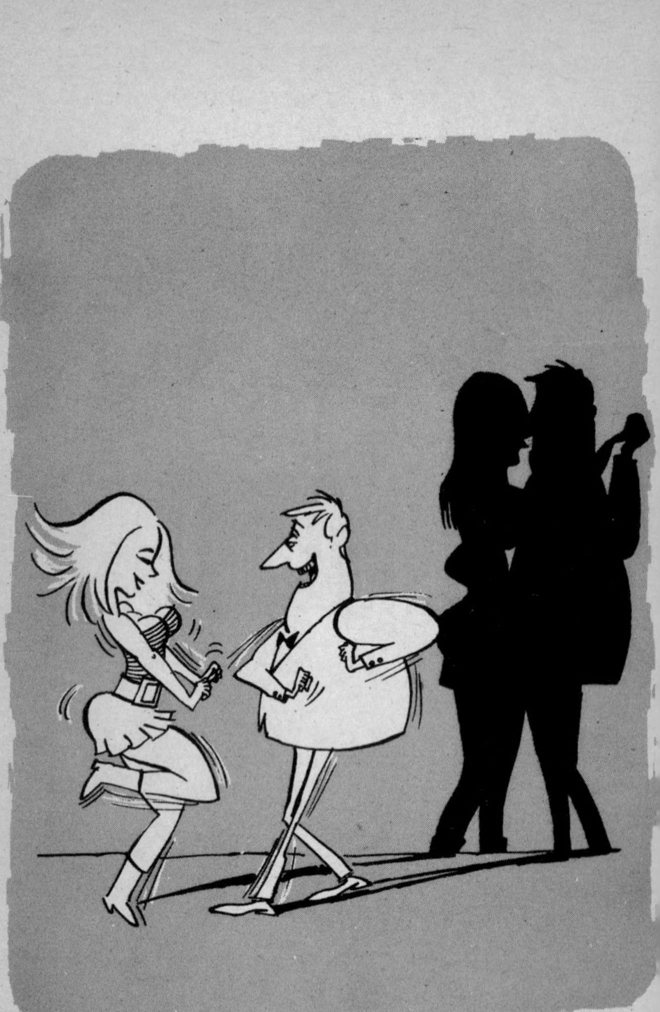

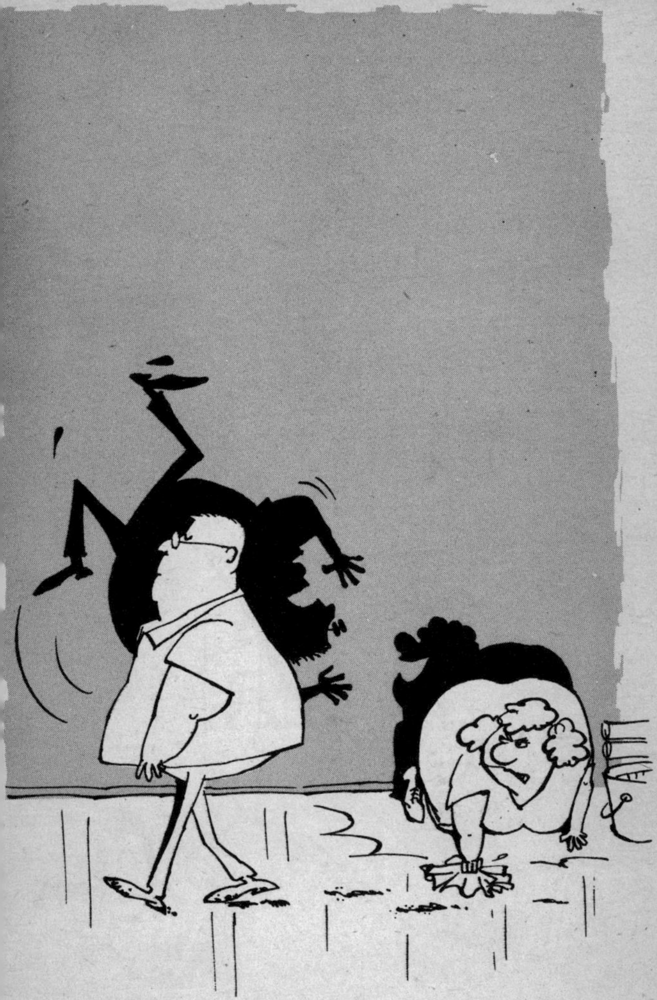

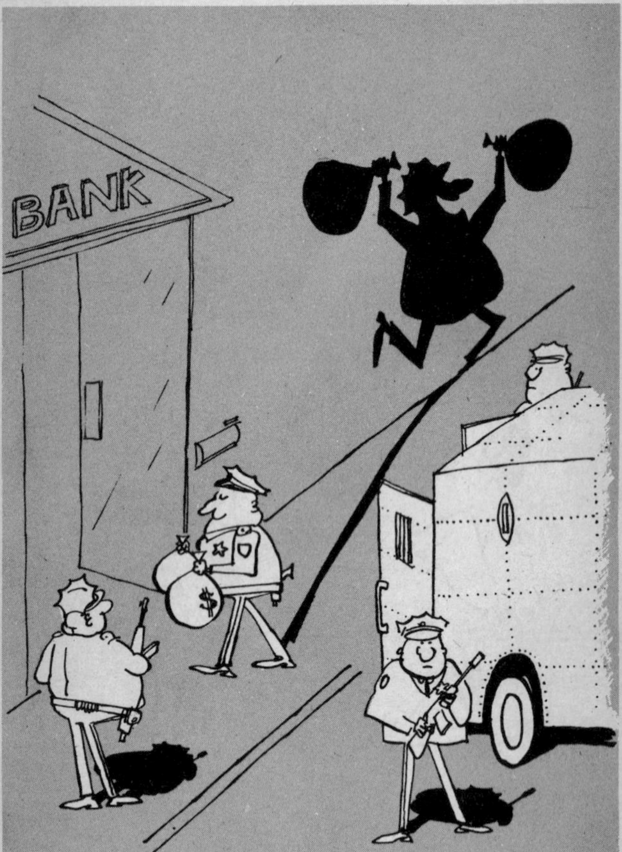
BANK

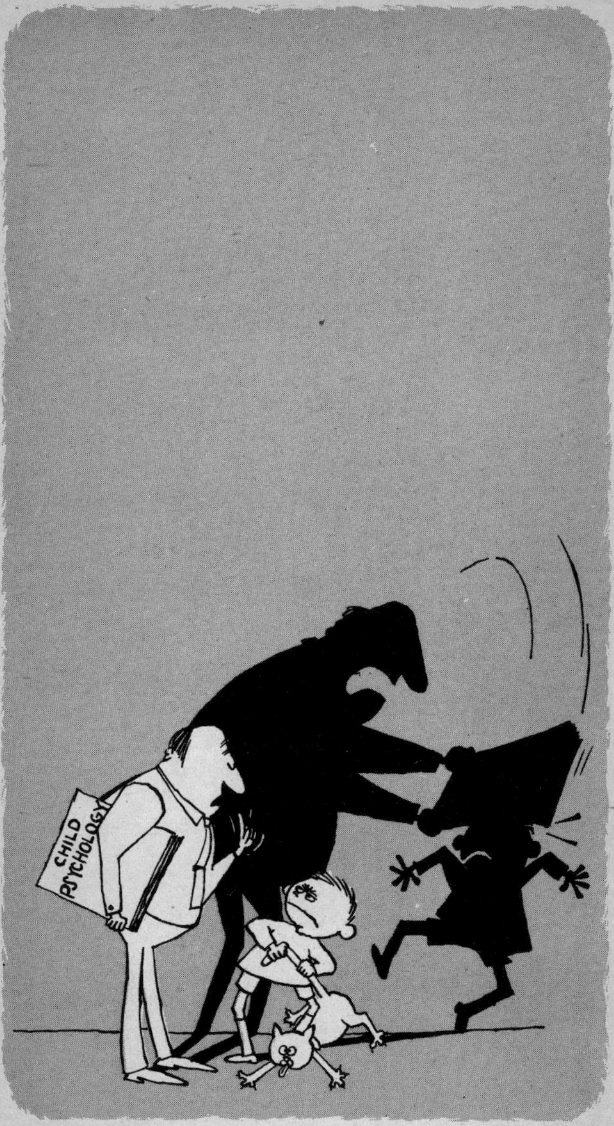
CHILD
PSYCHOLOGY

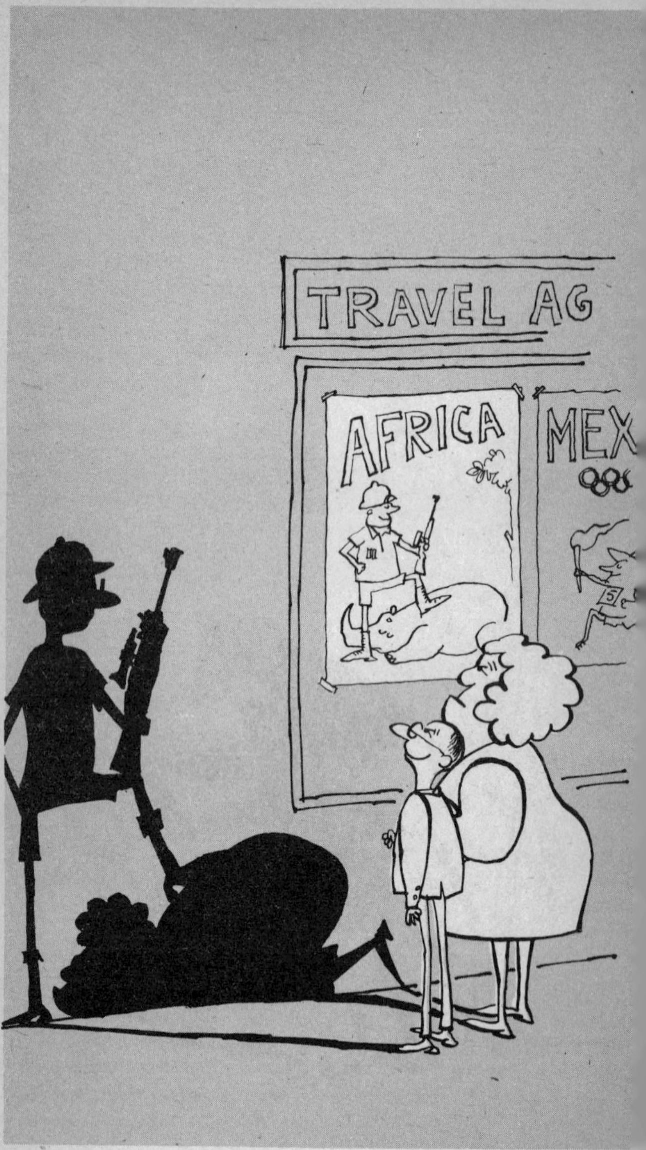
TRAVEL AG
AFRICA
MEX

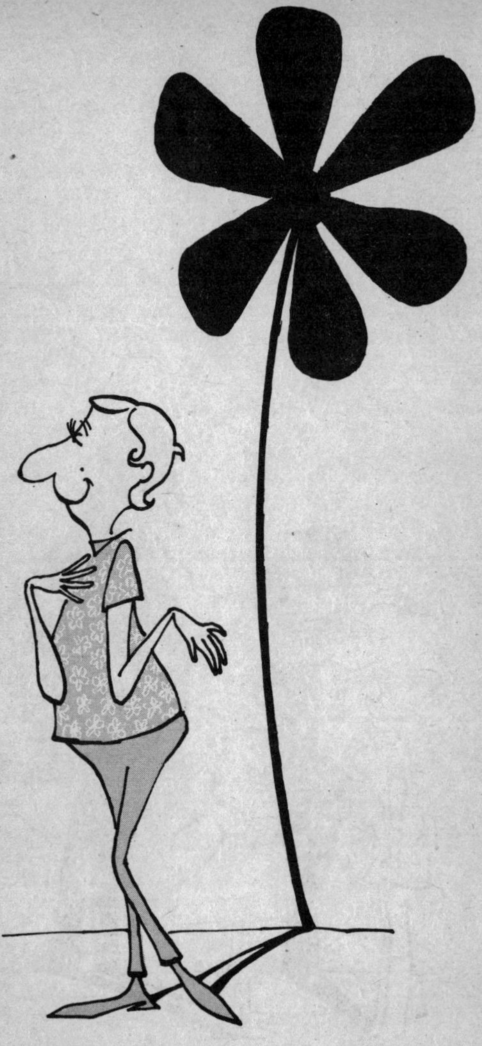

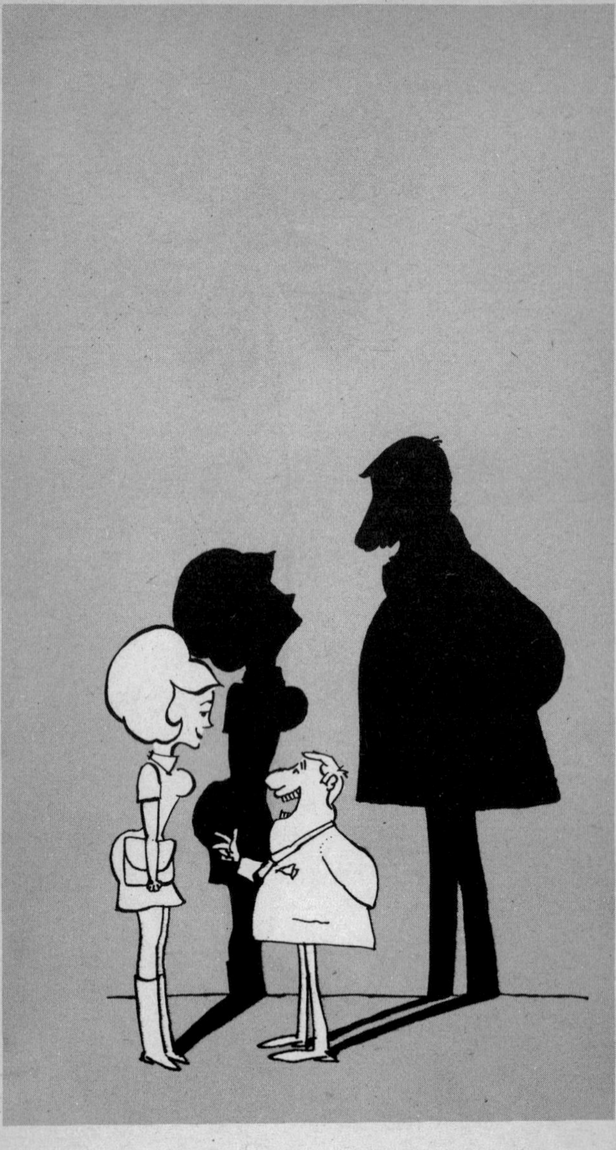

VIVA WATER SPORTS!

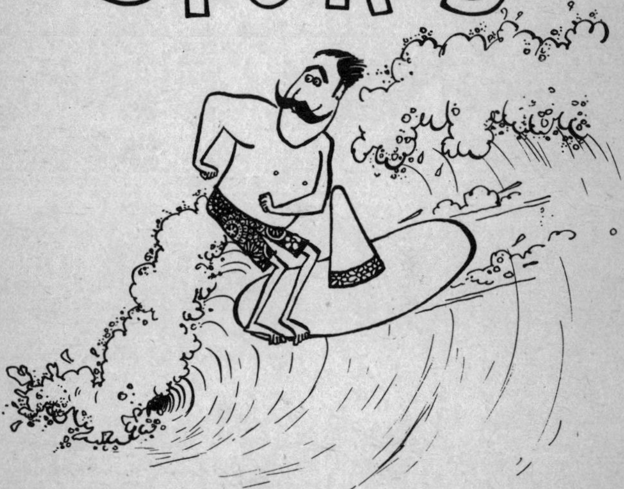

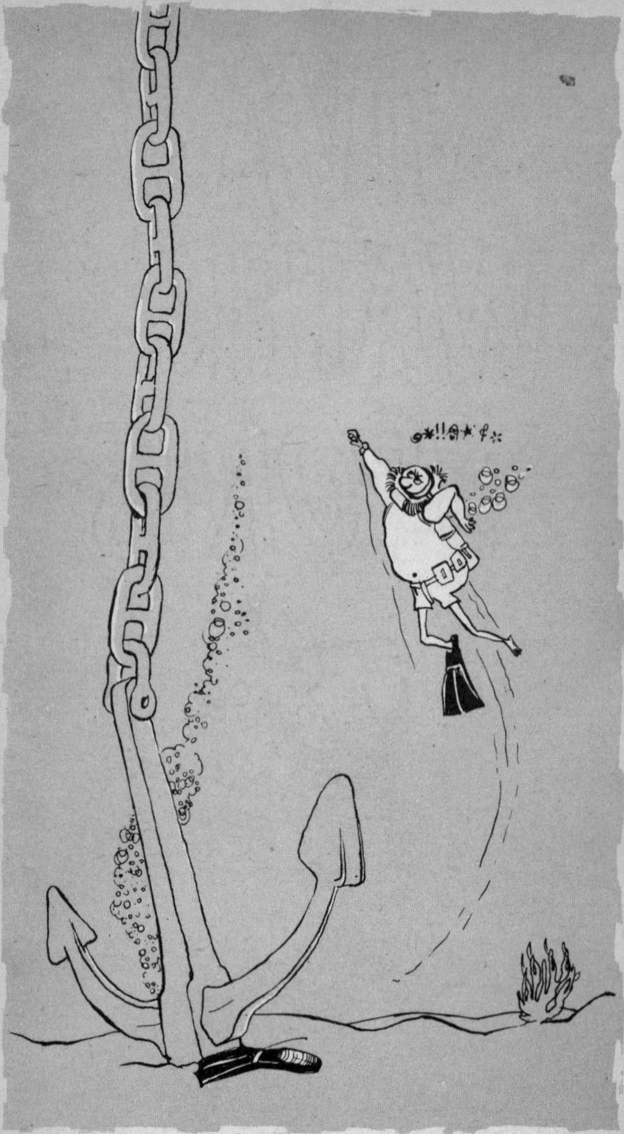

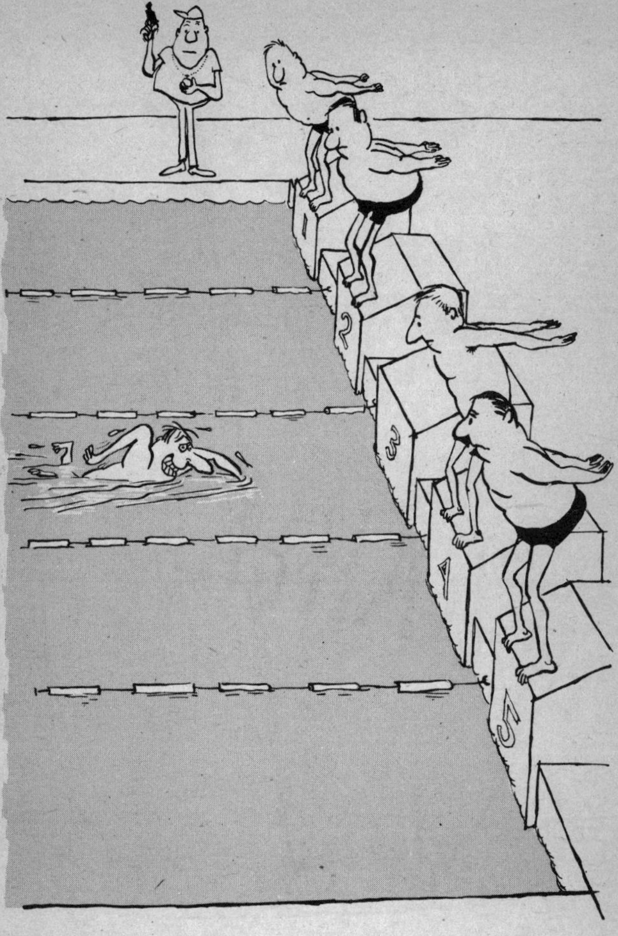
1
2
3
4
5

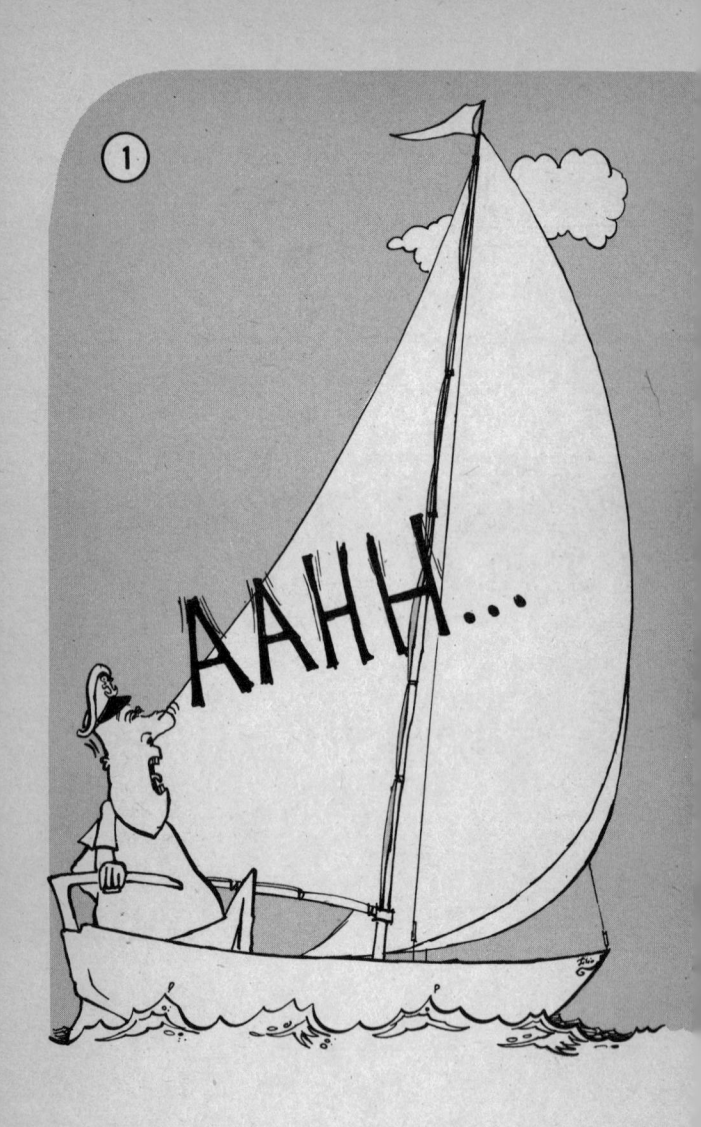
1
AAHH...

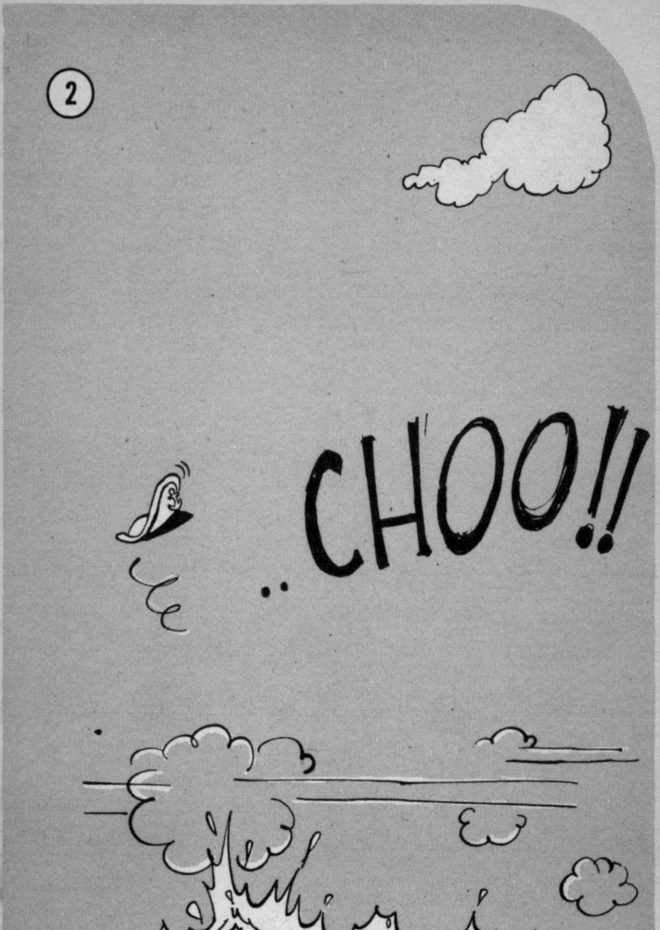
2
..CHOO!!

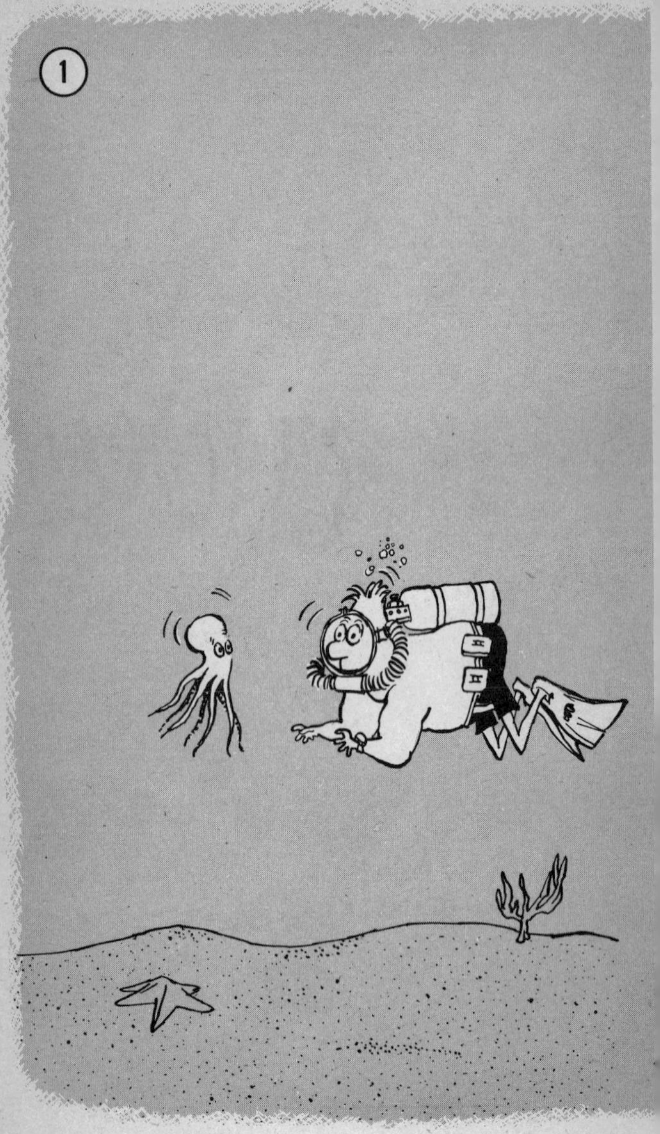

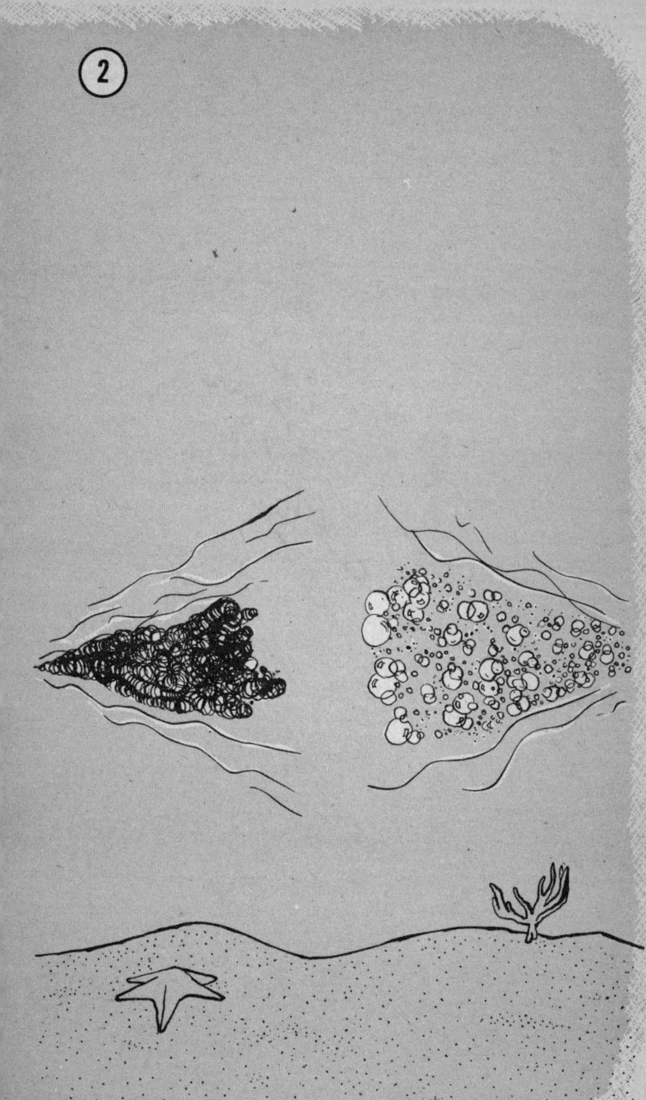
2

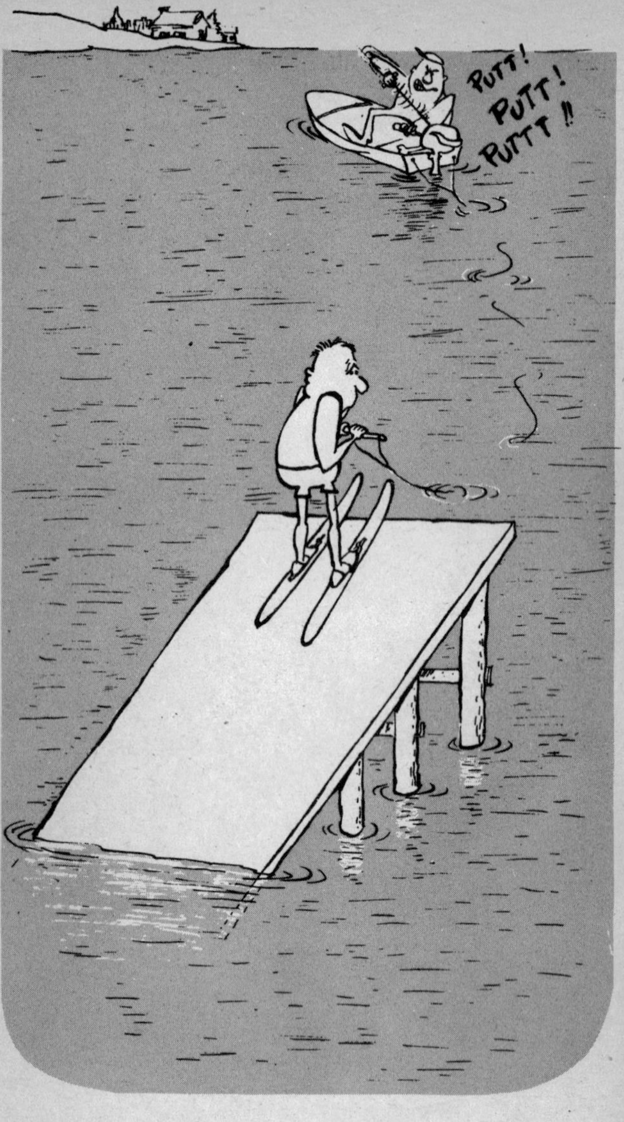
PUTT!
PUTT!
PUTTT!!

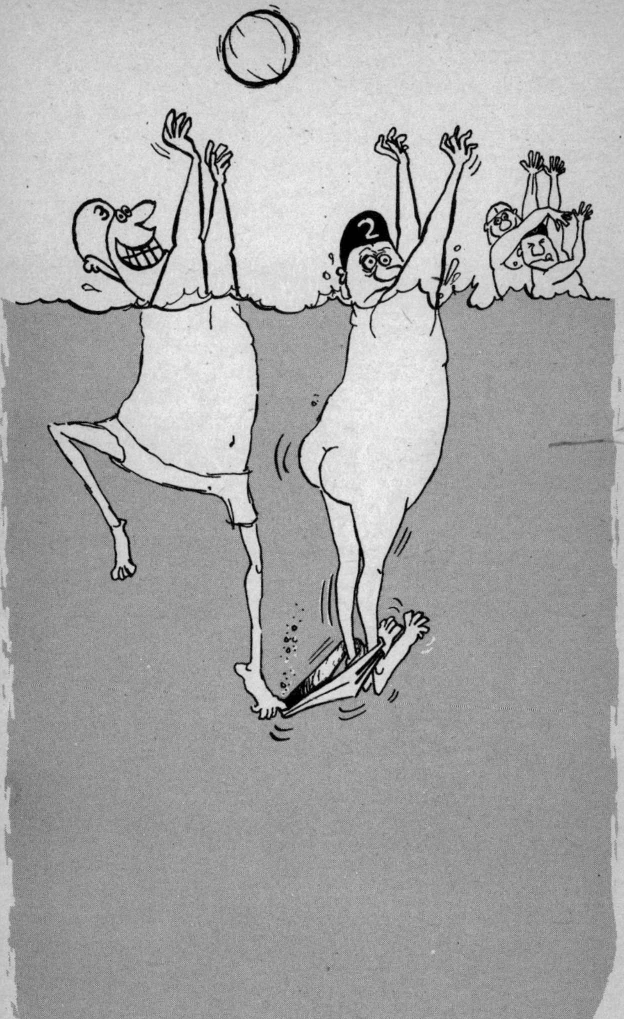

①

(2)

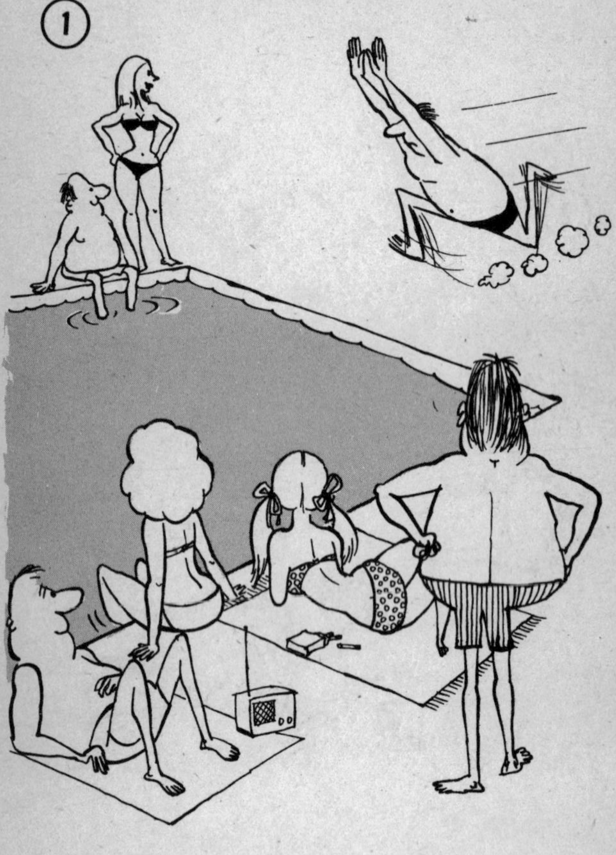
1

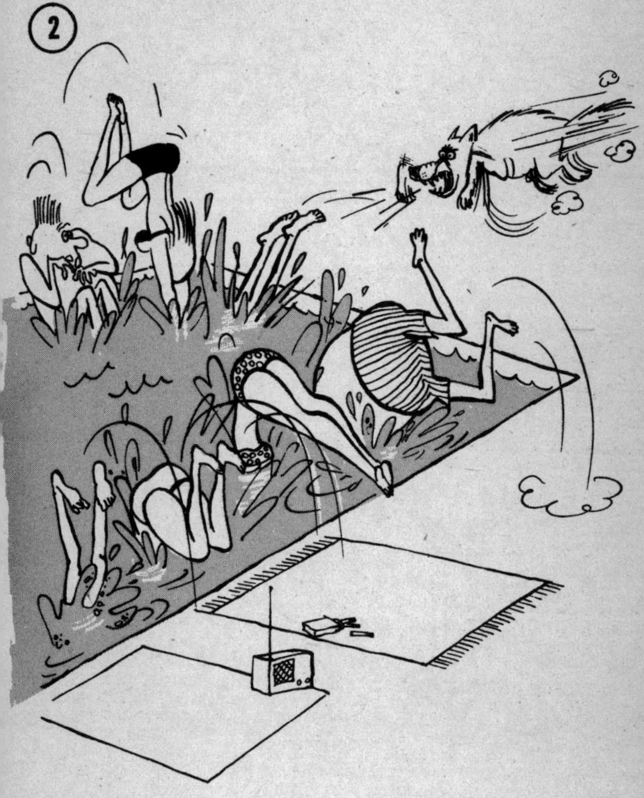
2

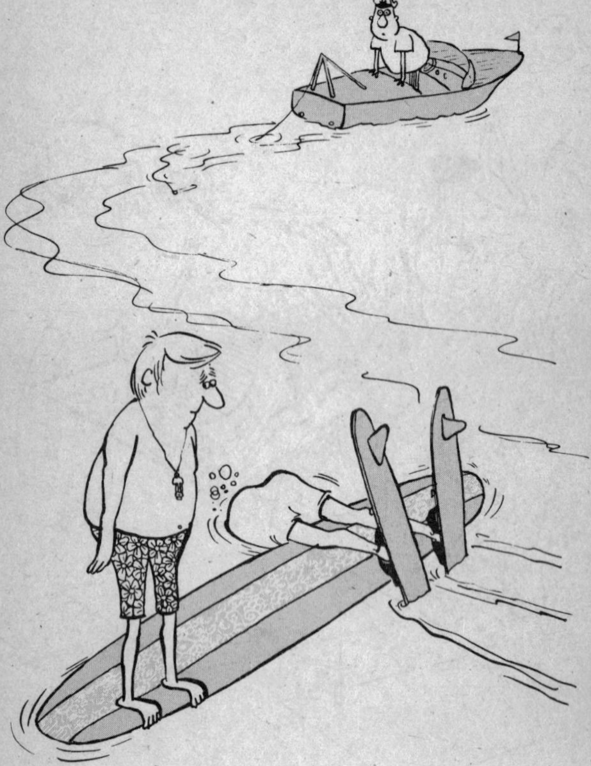

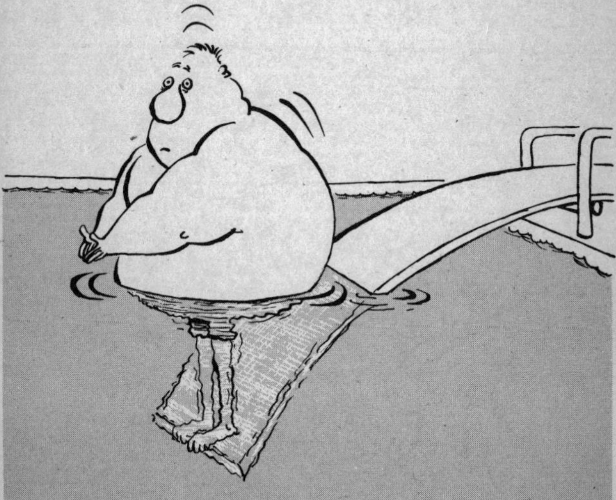

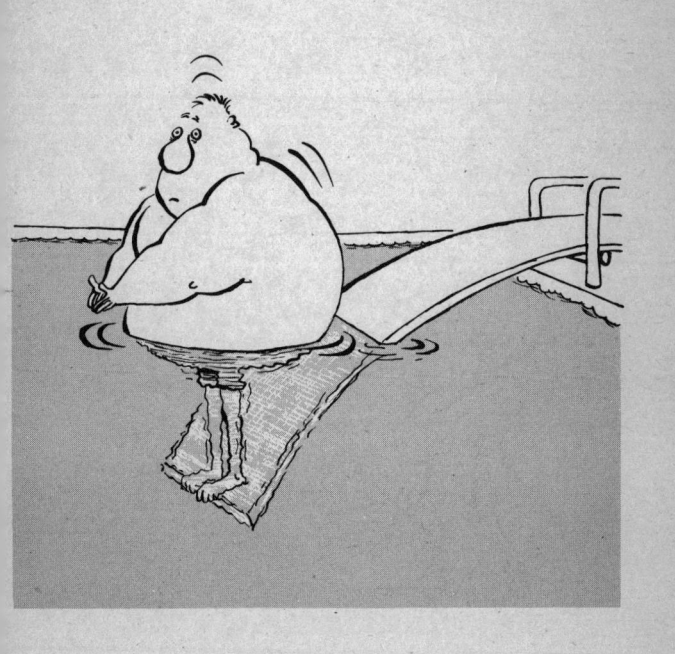

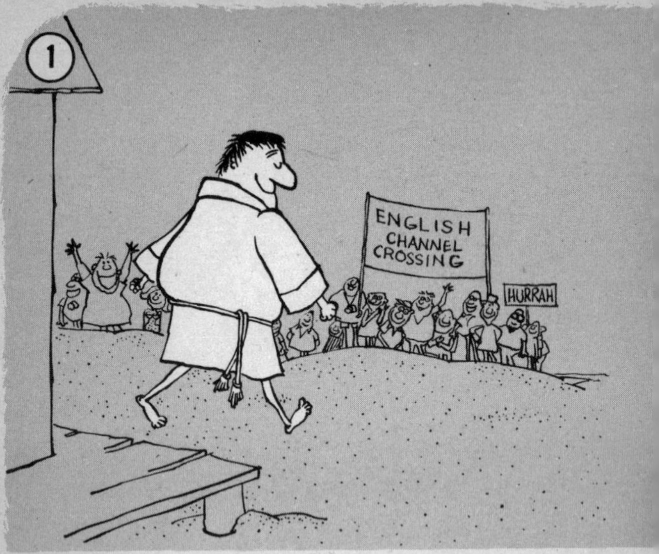
1
ENGLISH CHANNEL CROSSING
HURRAH

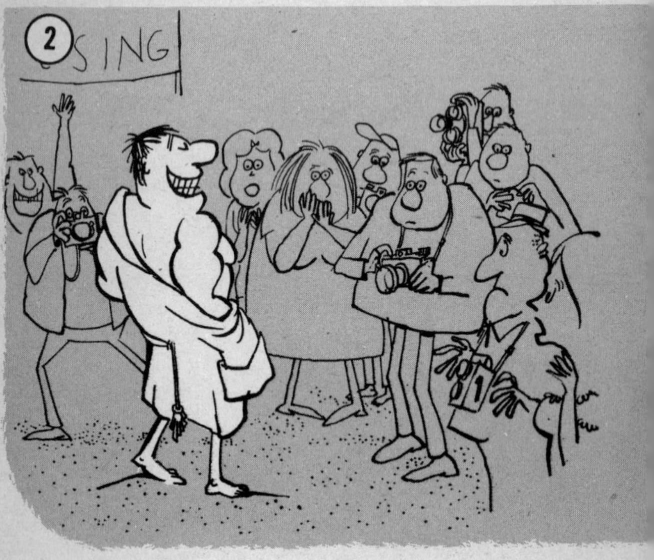
2
SING
1

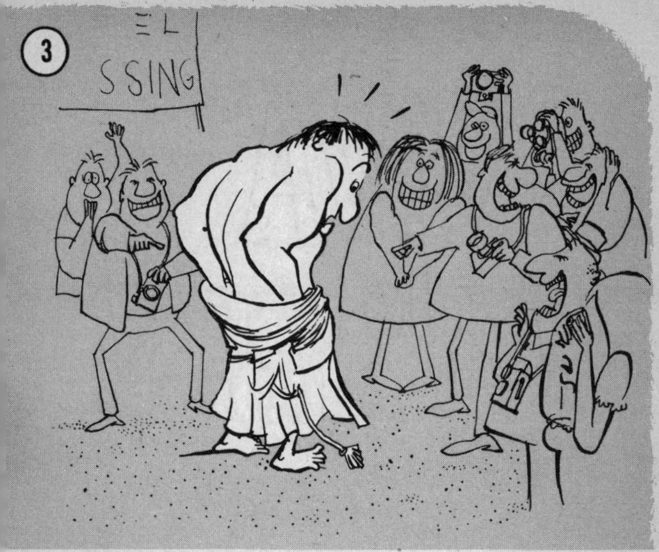
3
EL
SSING

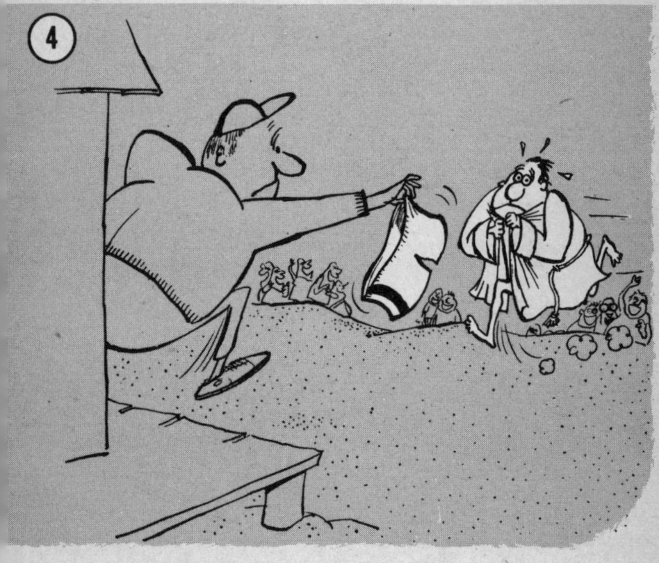
4

VIVA MONSTERS!

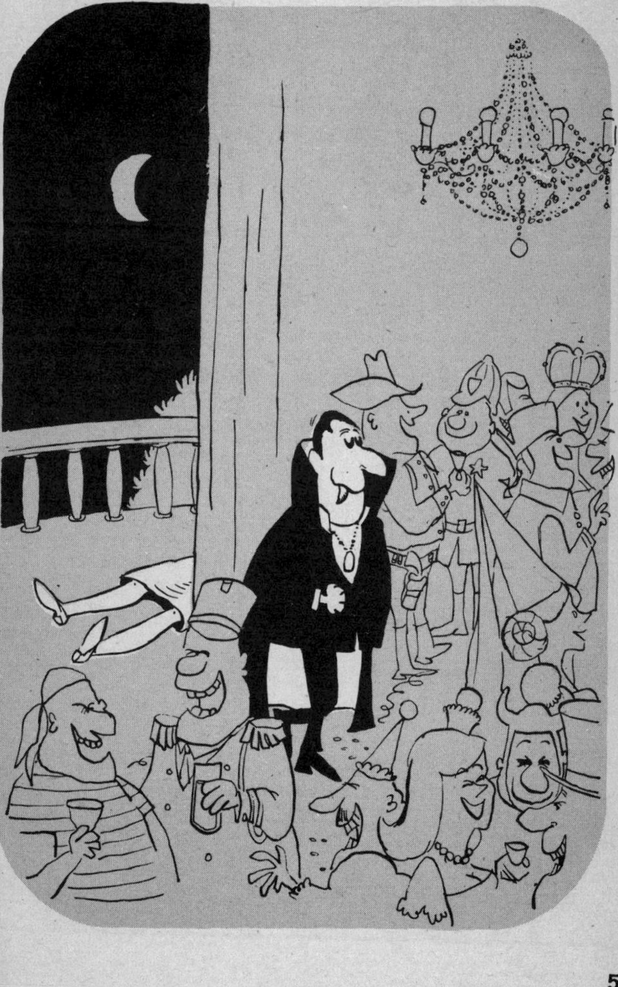

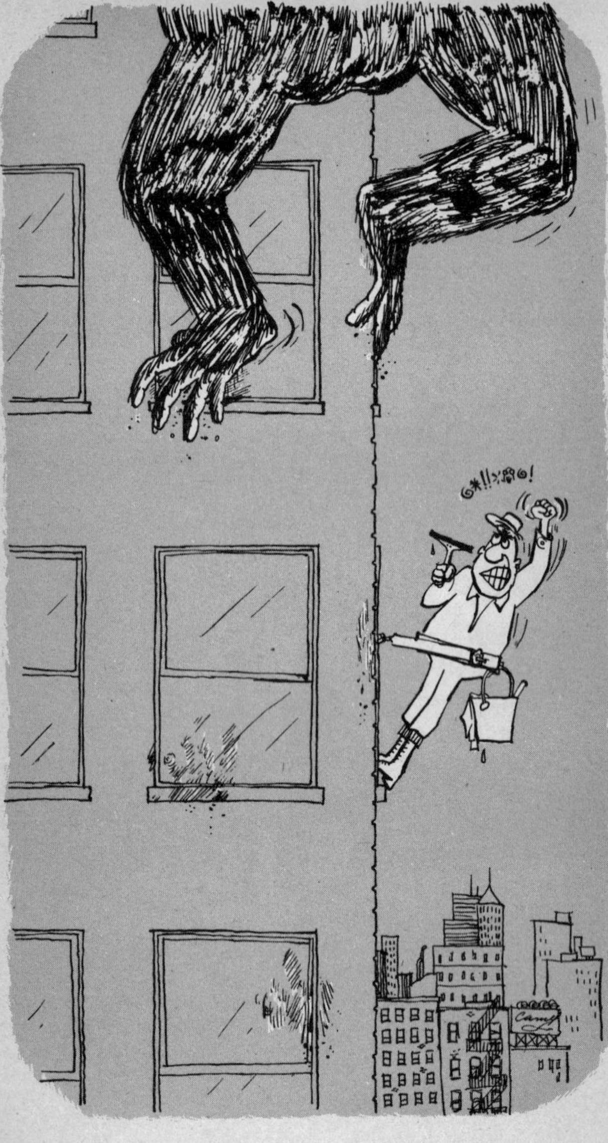

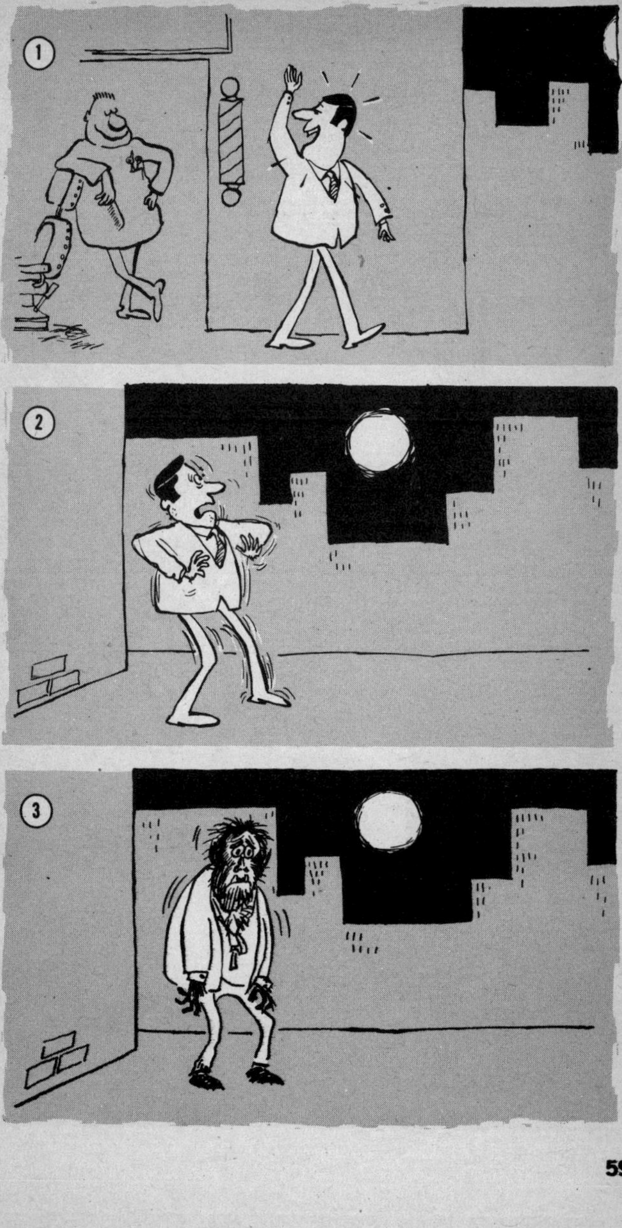
1
2
3

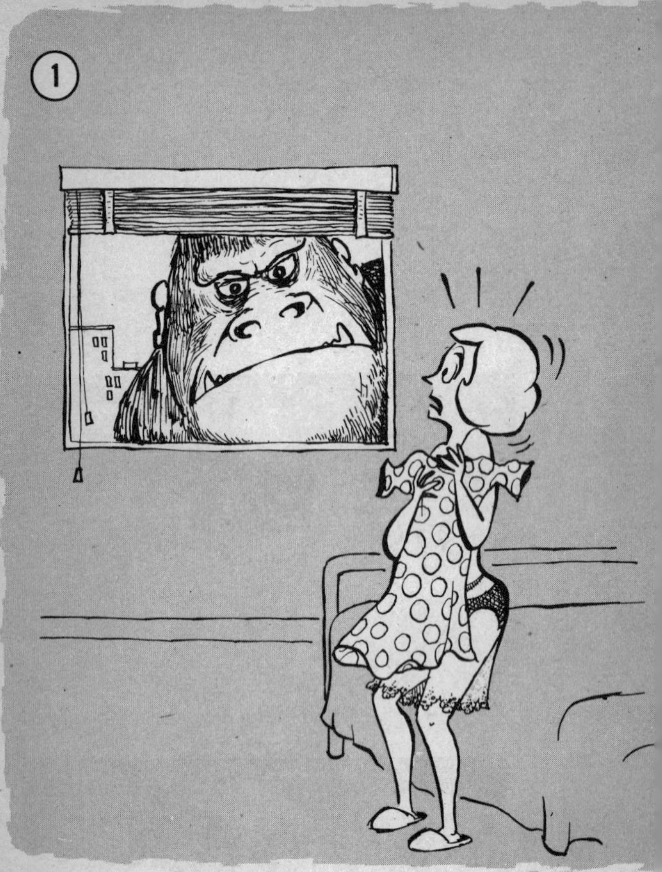
1

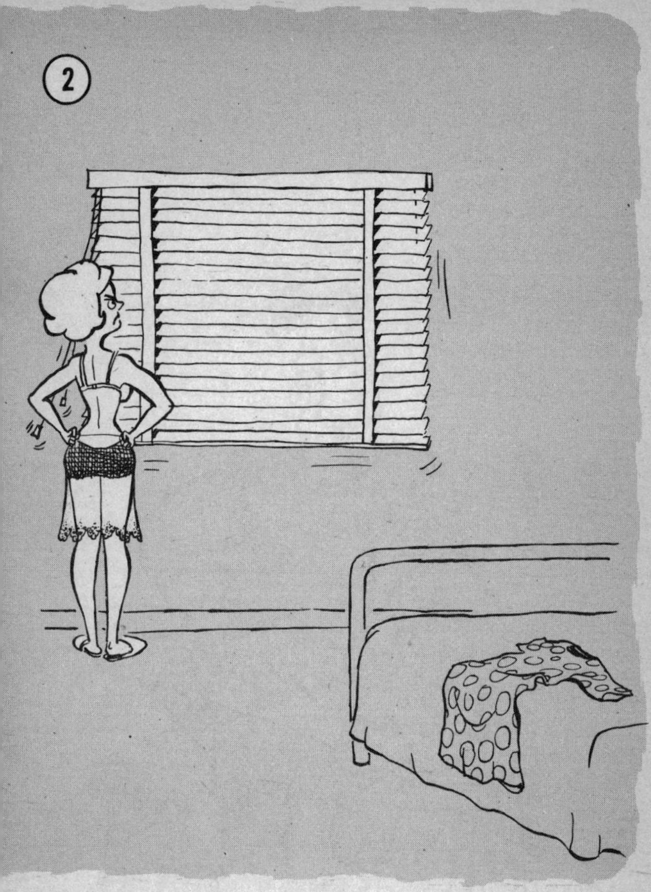
2

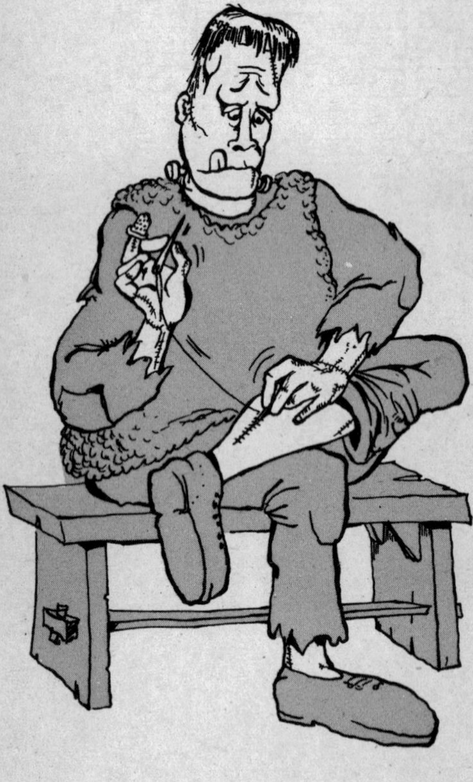

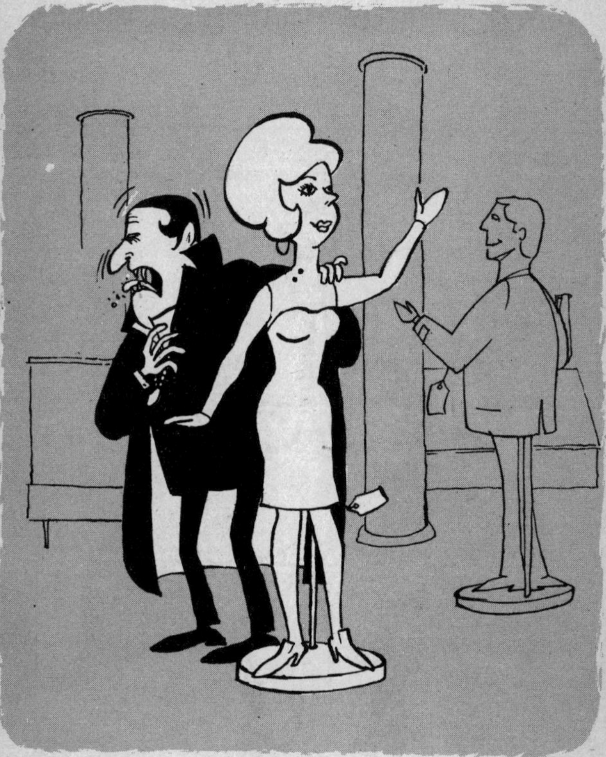

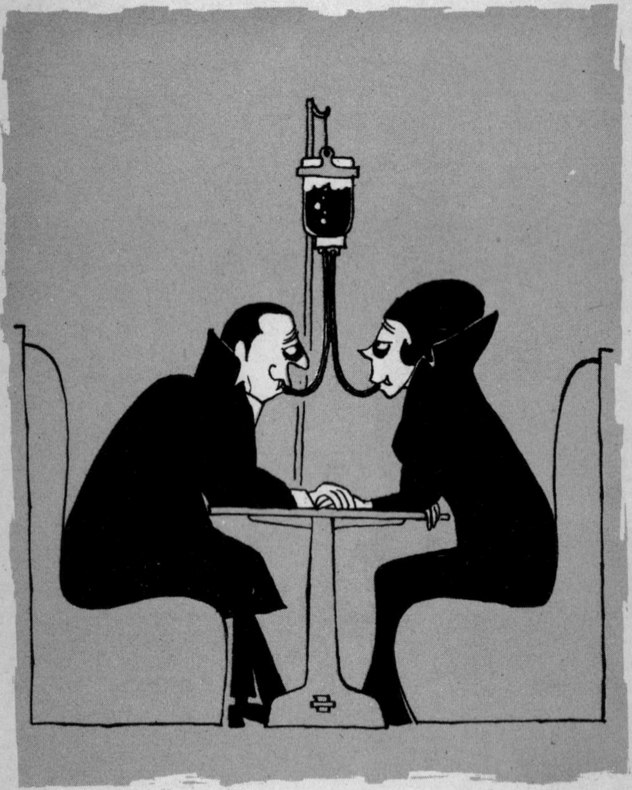

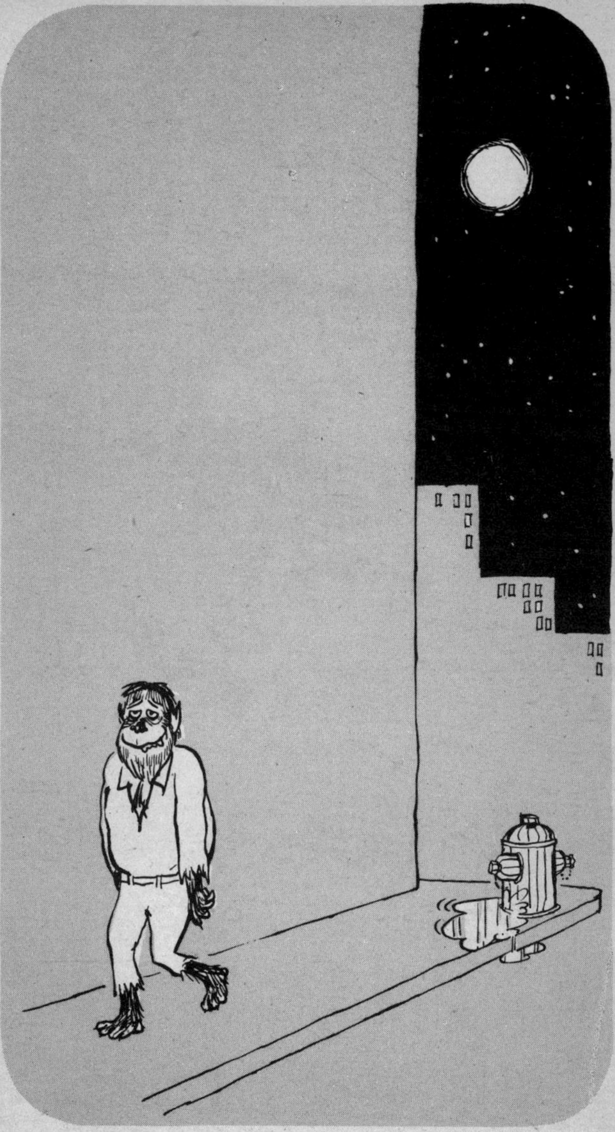

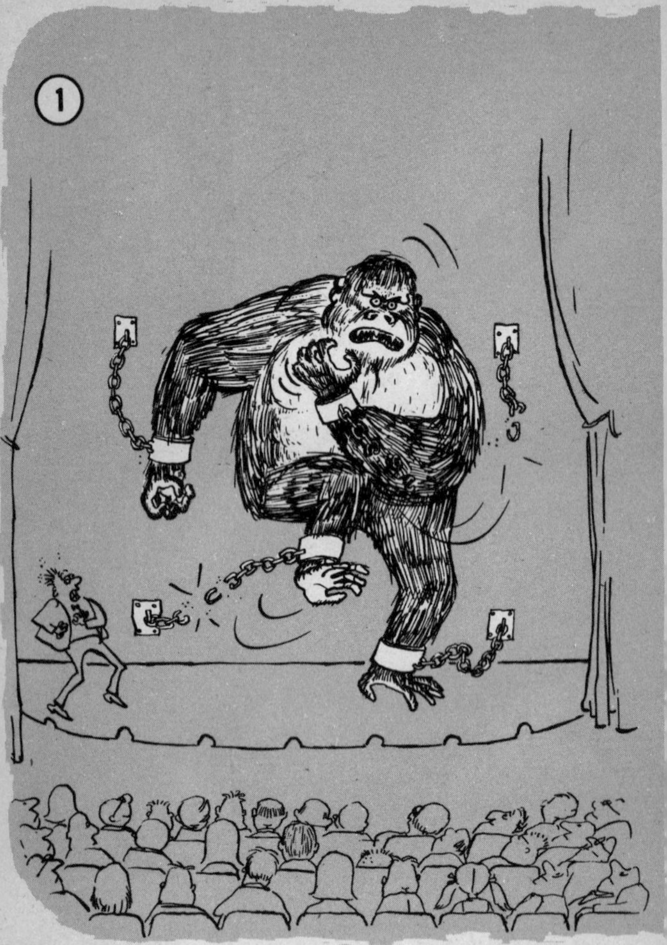
1

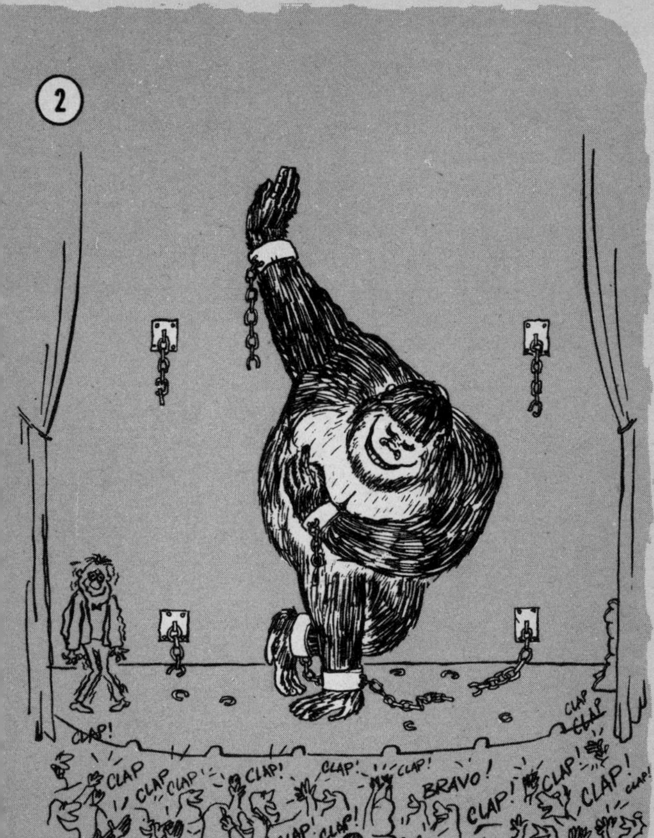
2
CLAP!
CLAP
CLAP
CLAP
CLAP!
CLAP!
CLAP!
BRAVO!
CLAP!
CLAP!
CLAP!
CLAP!
CLAP!
CLAP!
CLAP
CLAP
CLAP!
CLAP

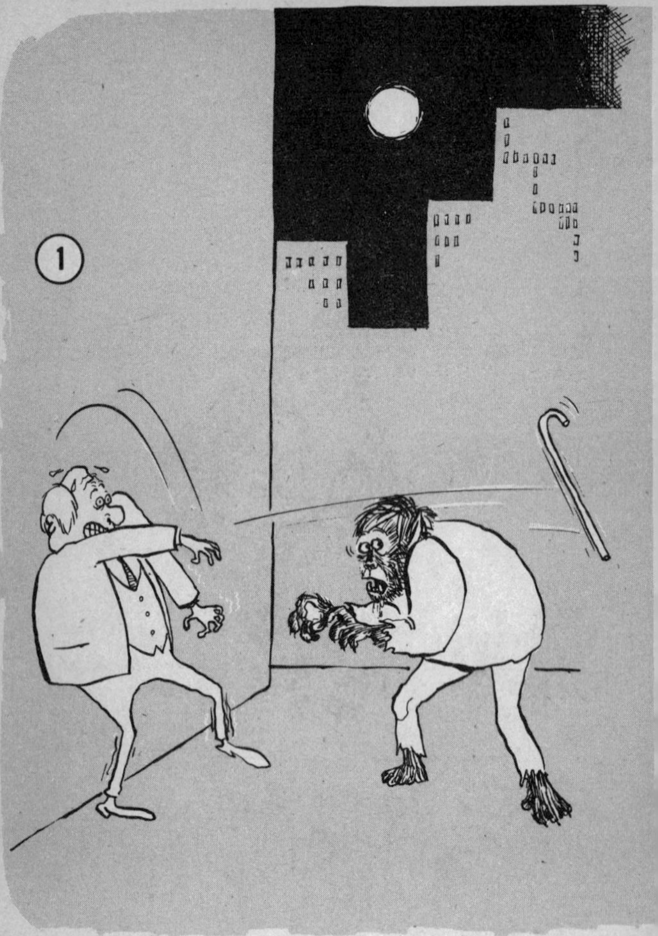

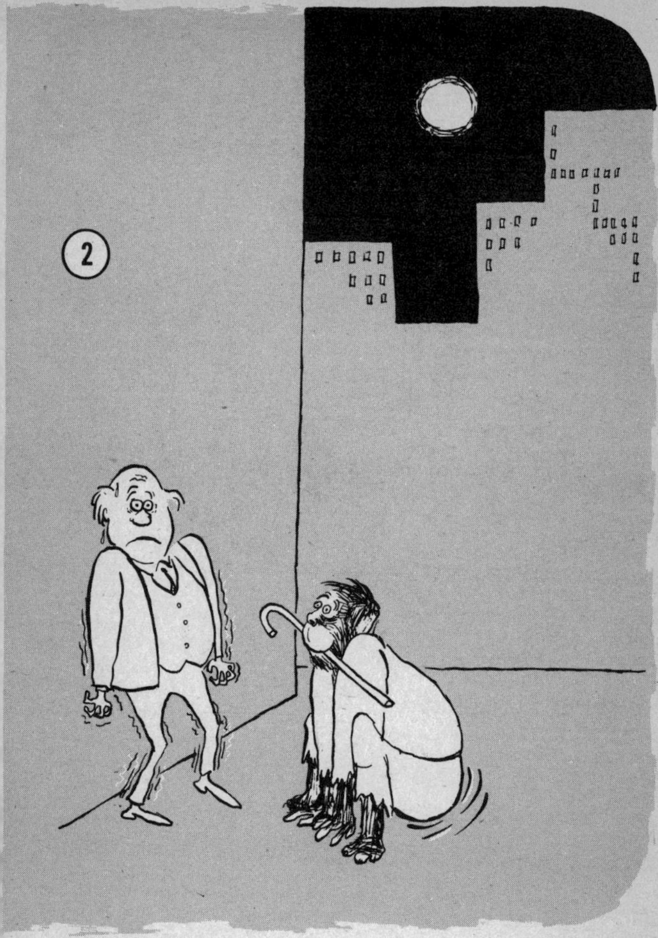
2

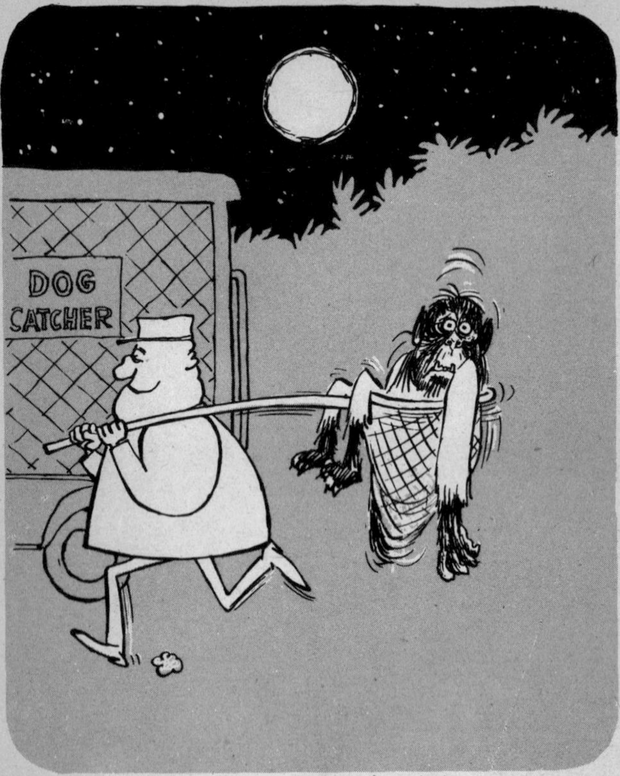
DOG
CATCHER

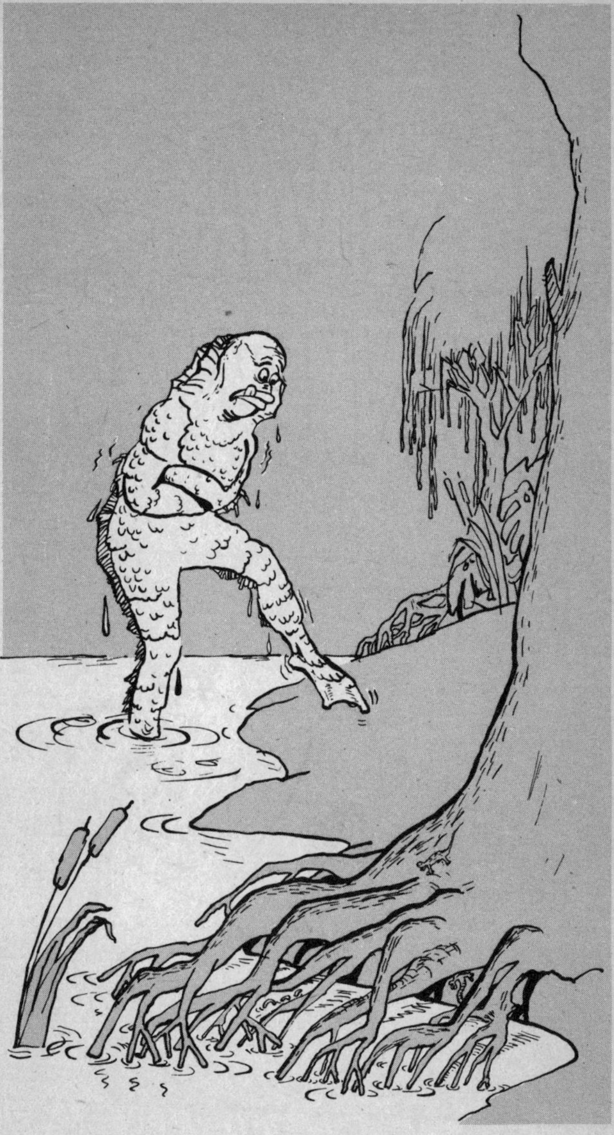

VIVA HUNTING!

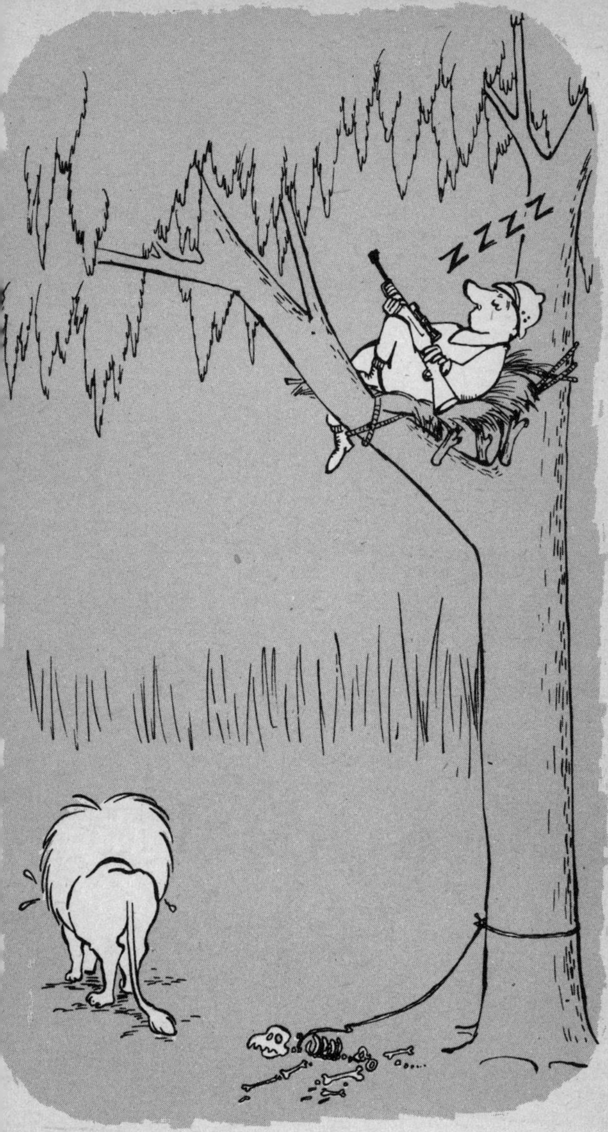
ZZZZ

74

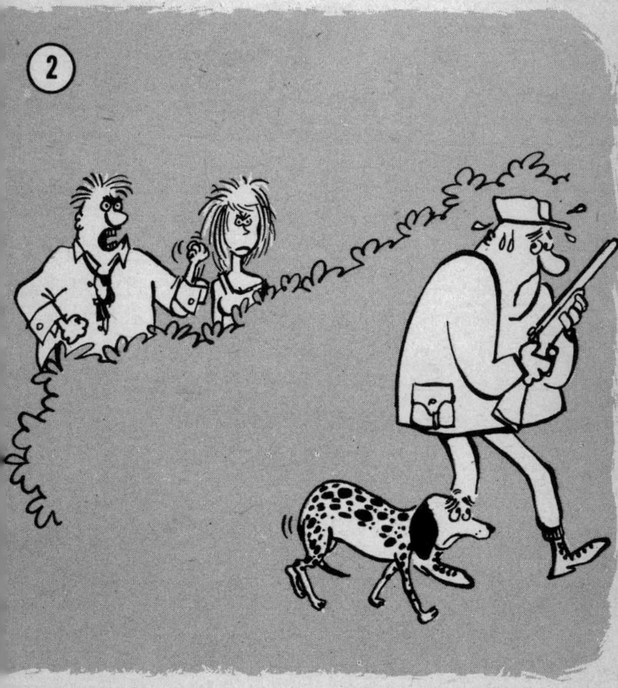
2

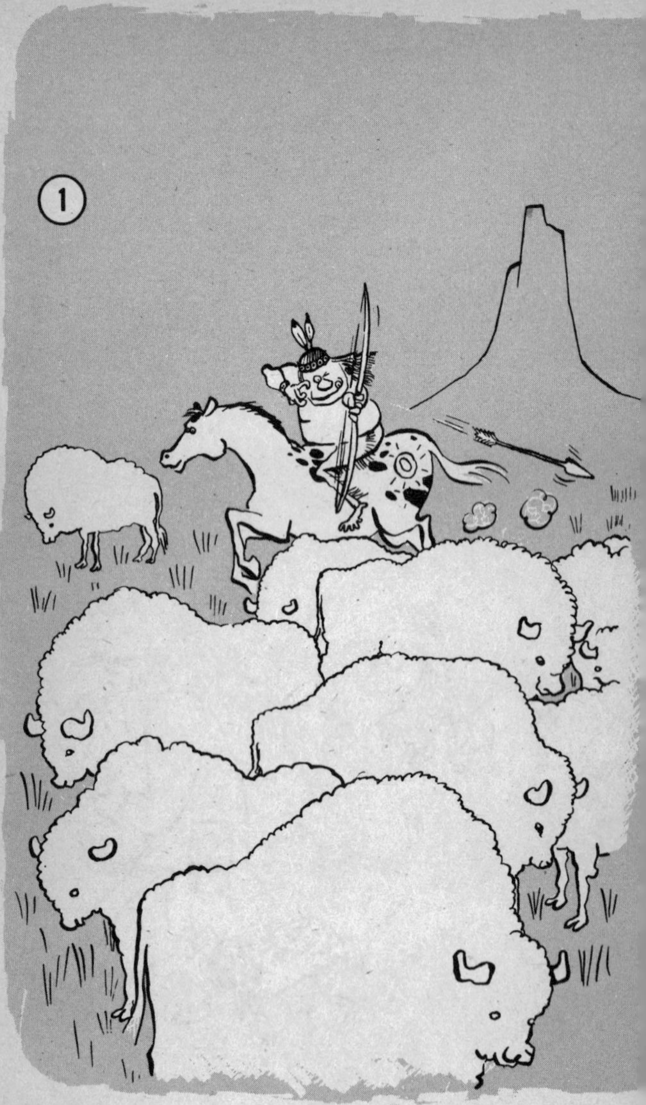
1

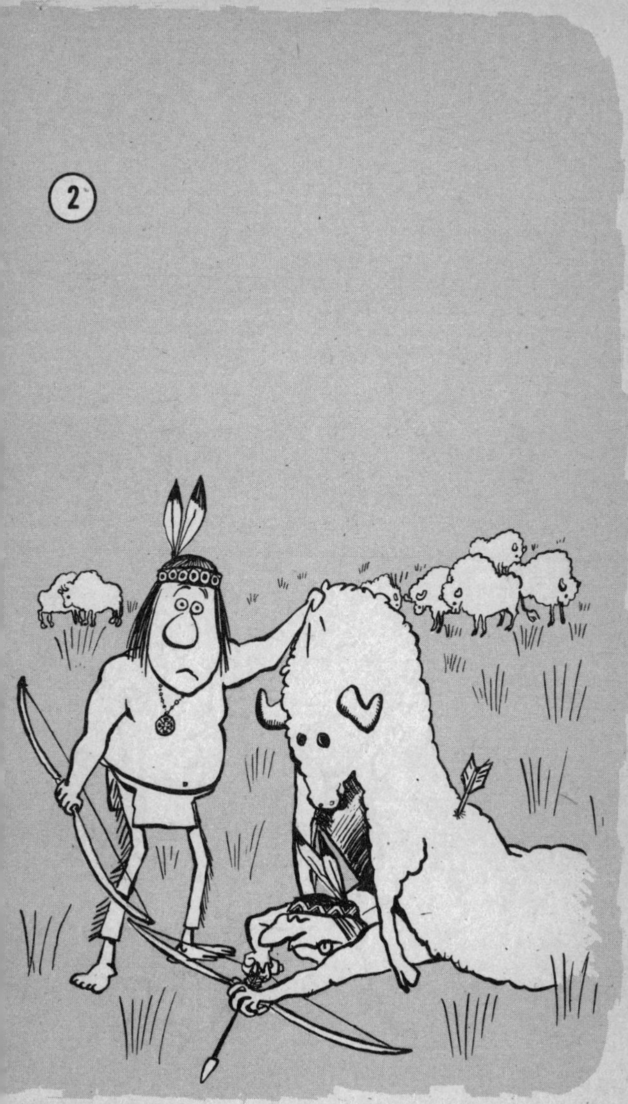
2

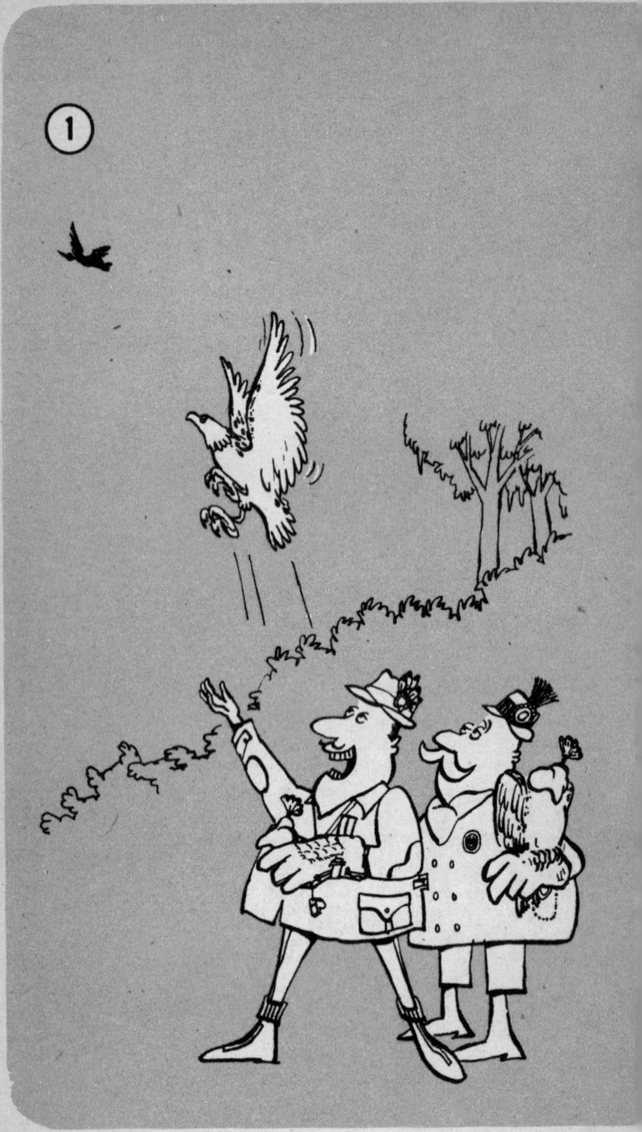
1

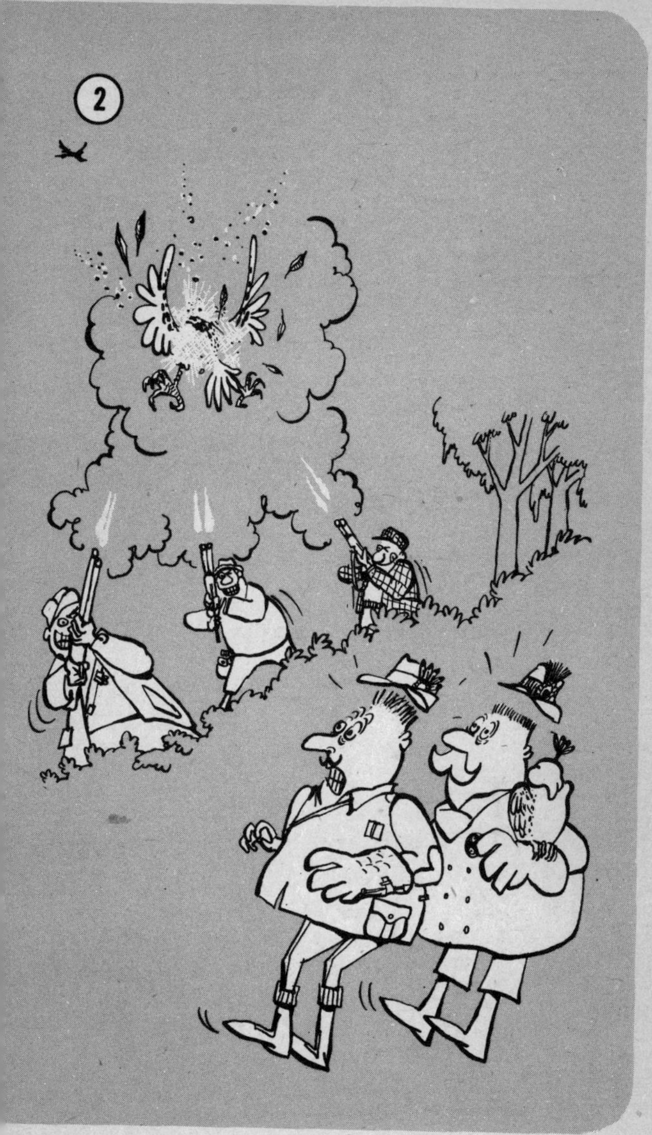
2

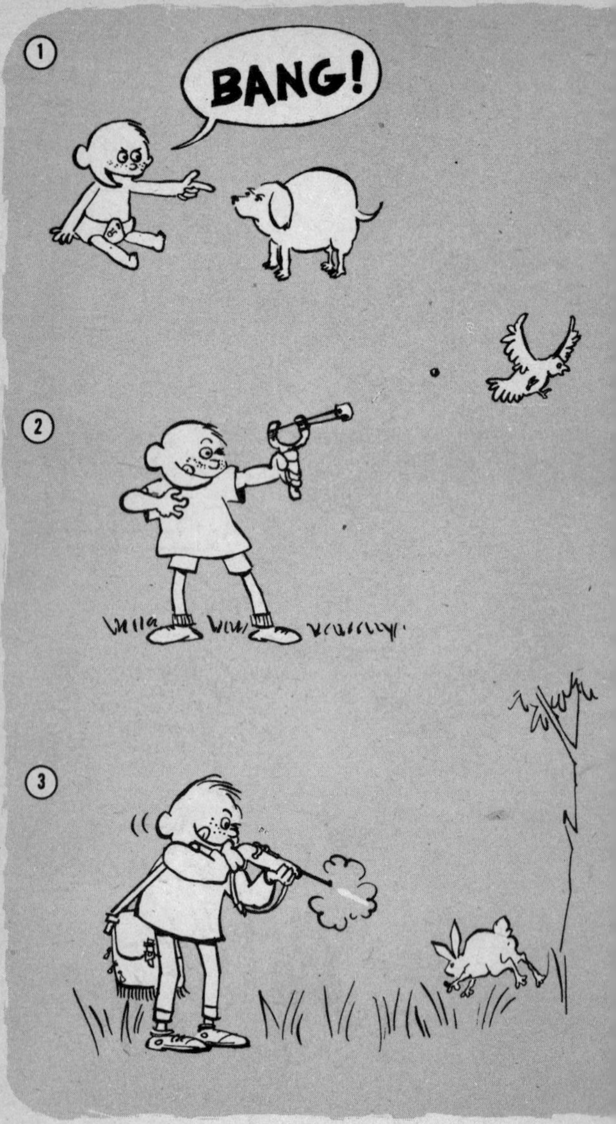
1
BANG!
2
3

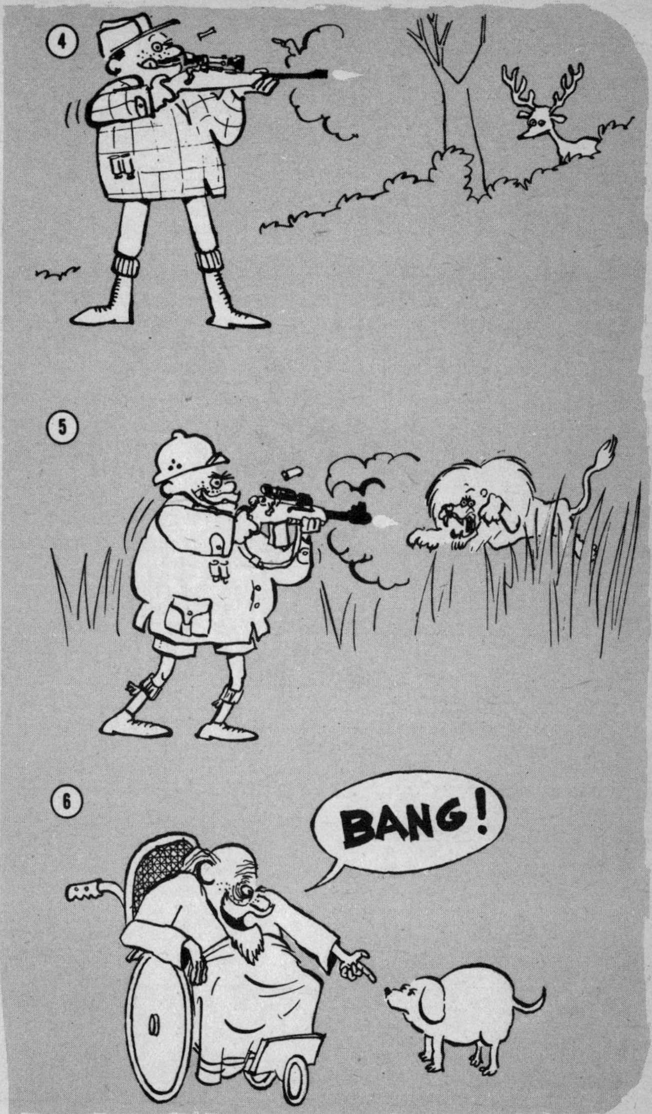
4
5
6
BANG!

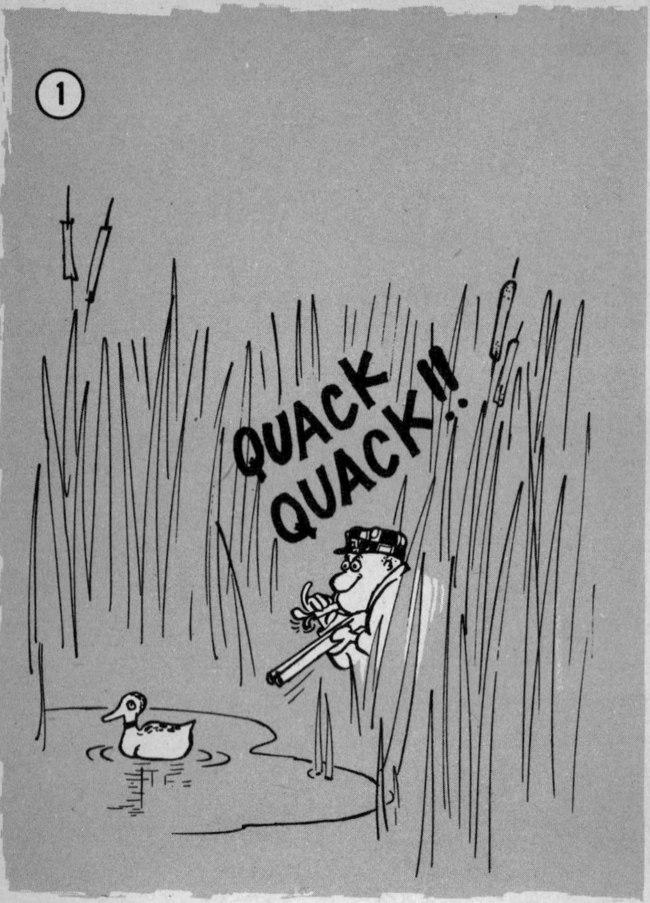
1
QUACK QUACK!!

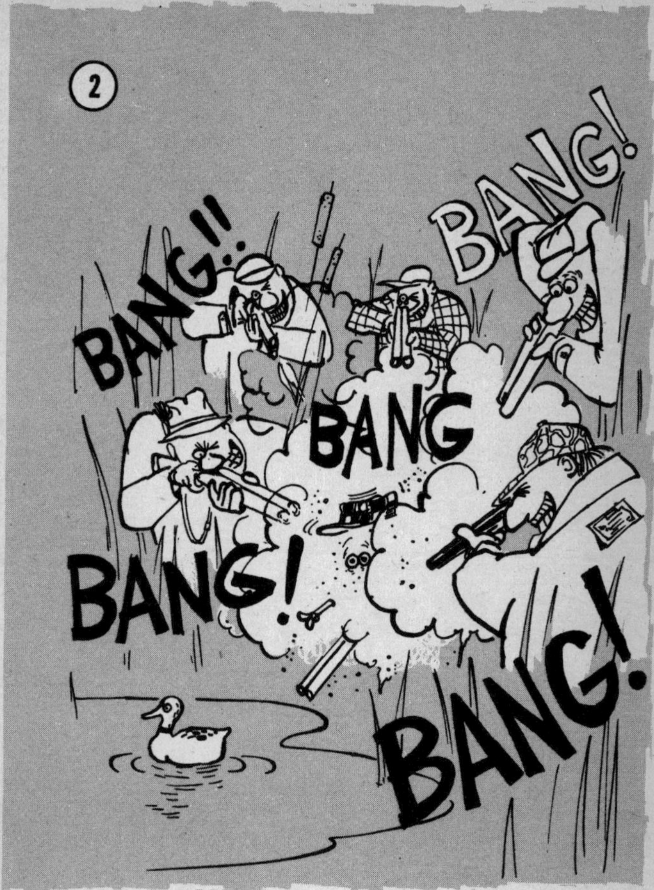
2
BANG!!
BANG!
BANG
BANG!
BANG!

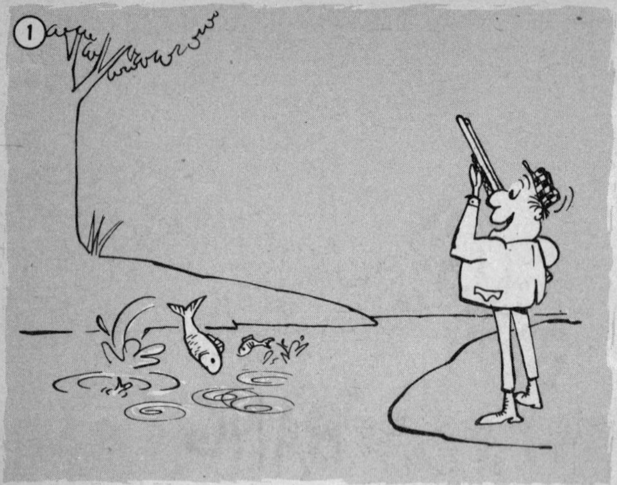
1

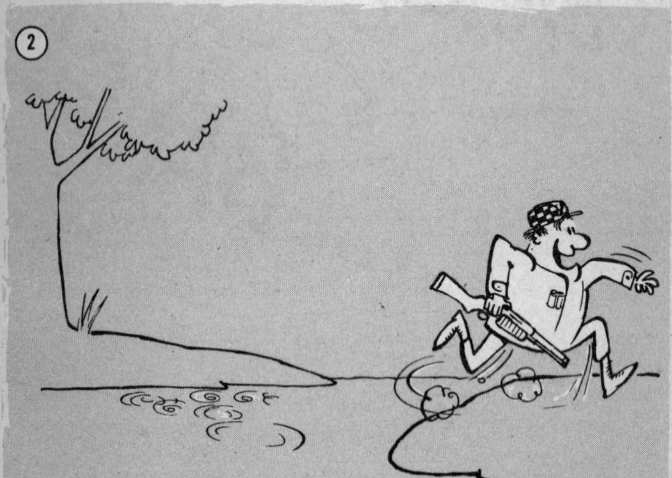
2

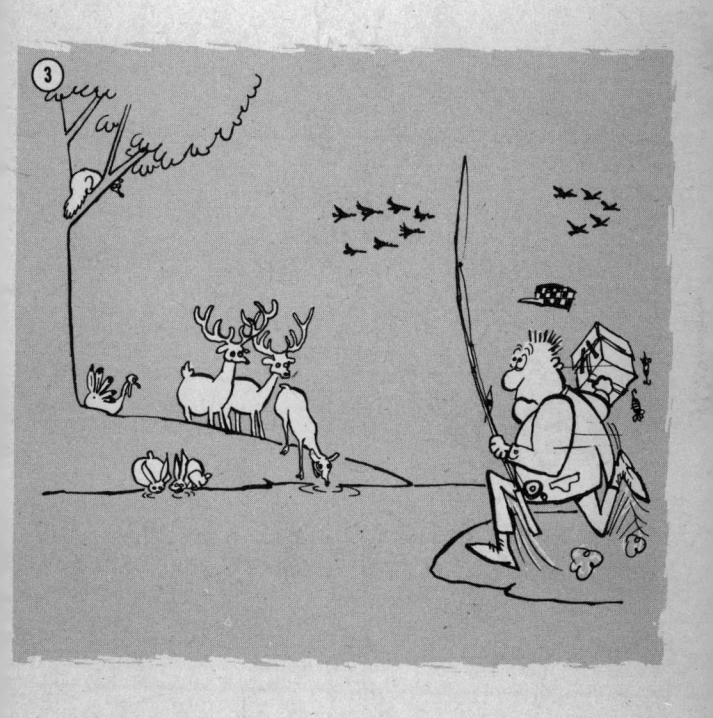
3

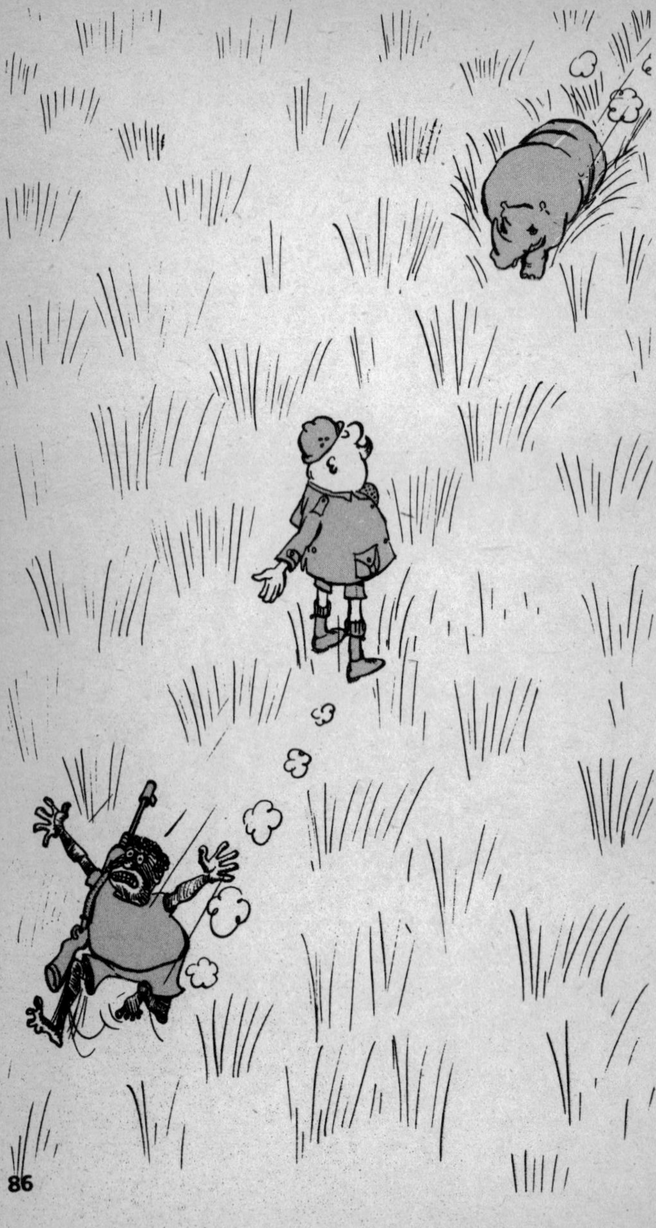

VIVA COPS & ROBBERS!

CUSTOMS
CIGARROS
CIGARROS

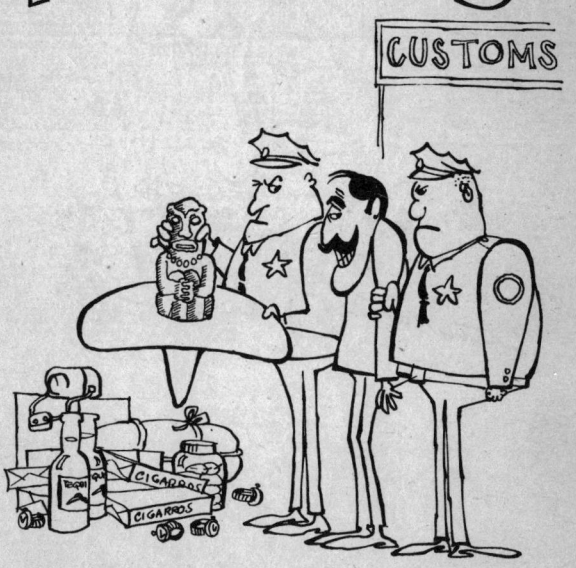

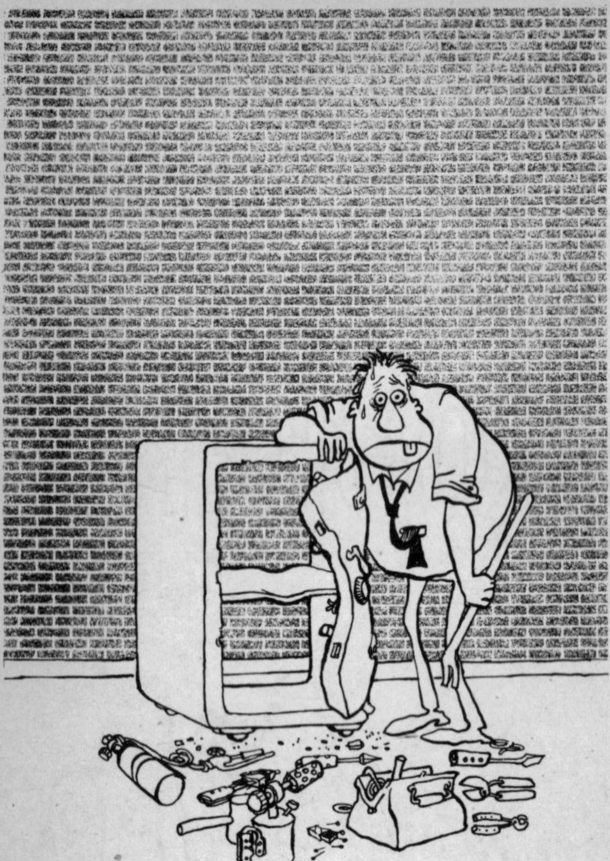

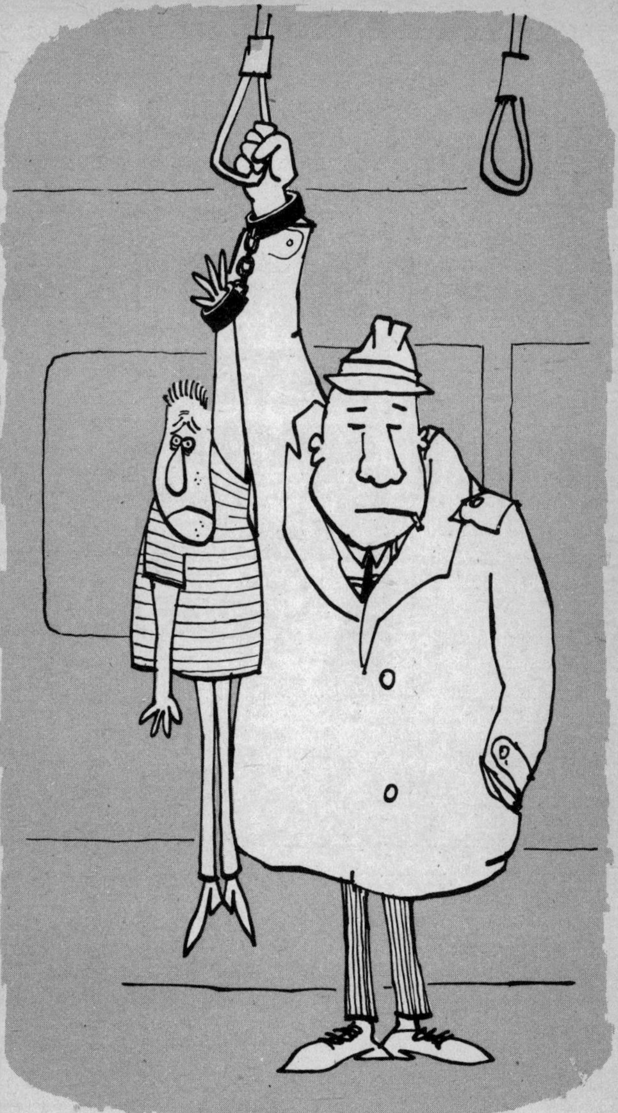

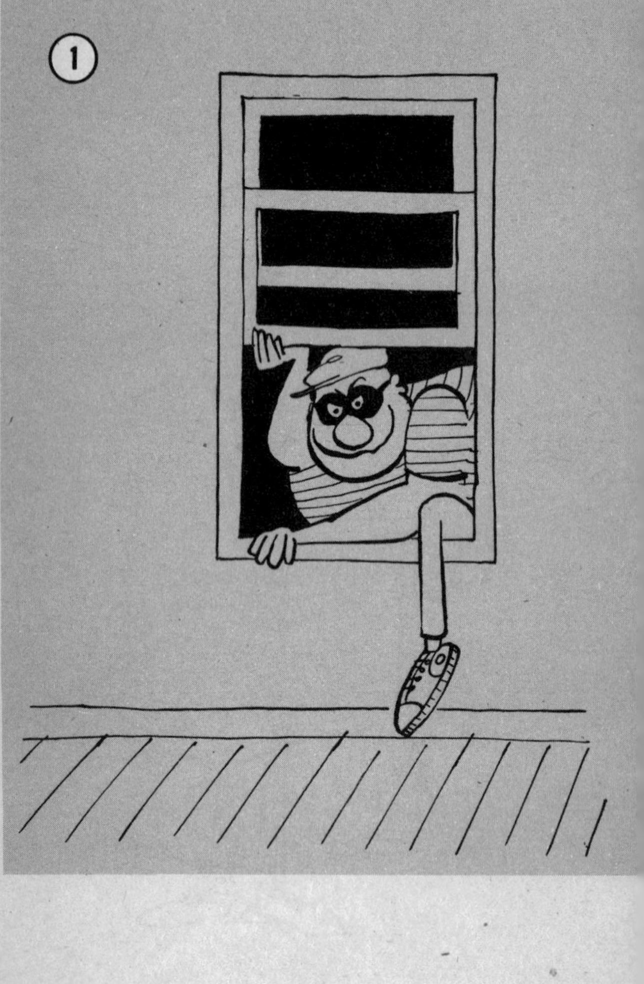
1

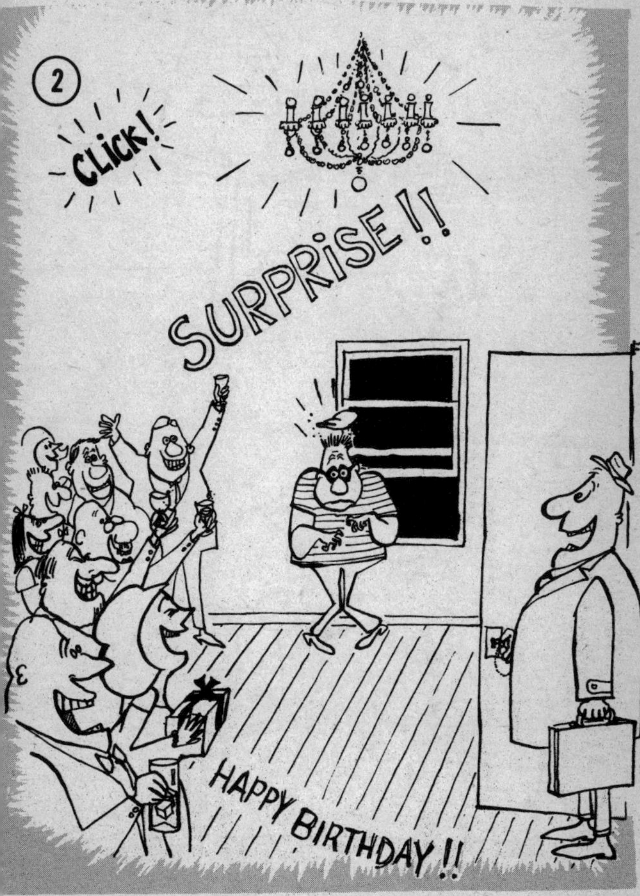
2
CLICK!
SURPRISE!!
HAPPY BIRTHDAY!!

(1)

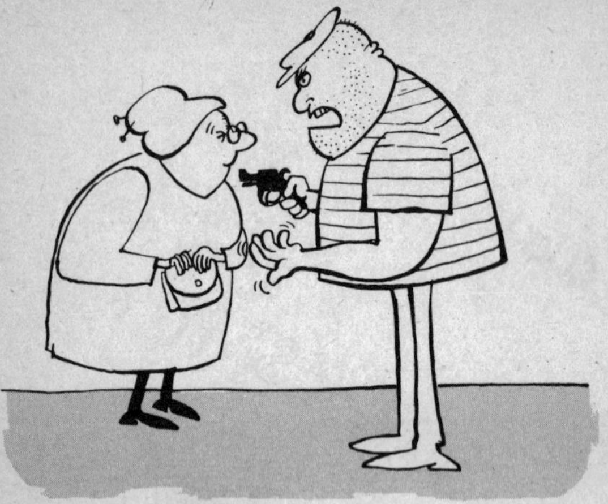

(2)

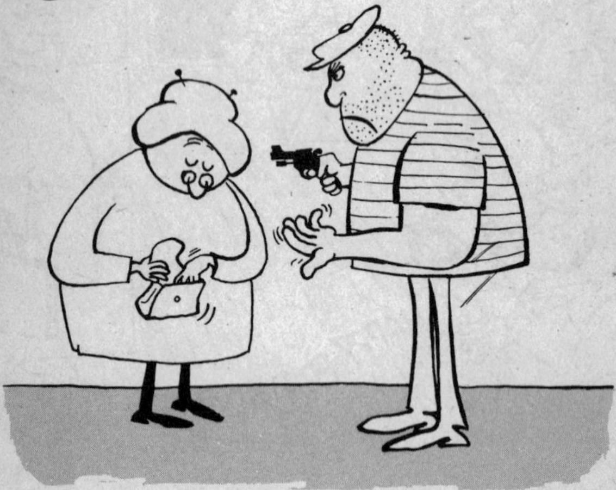

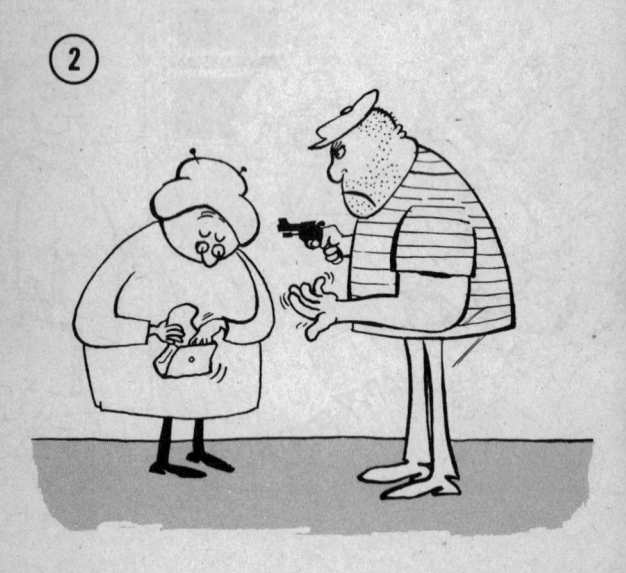

(3)

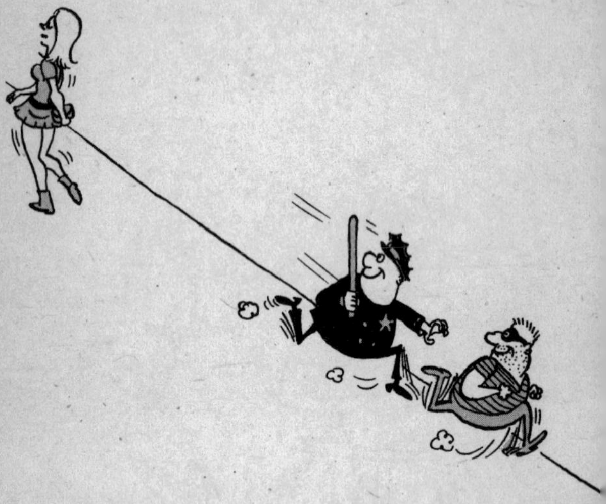

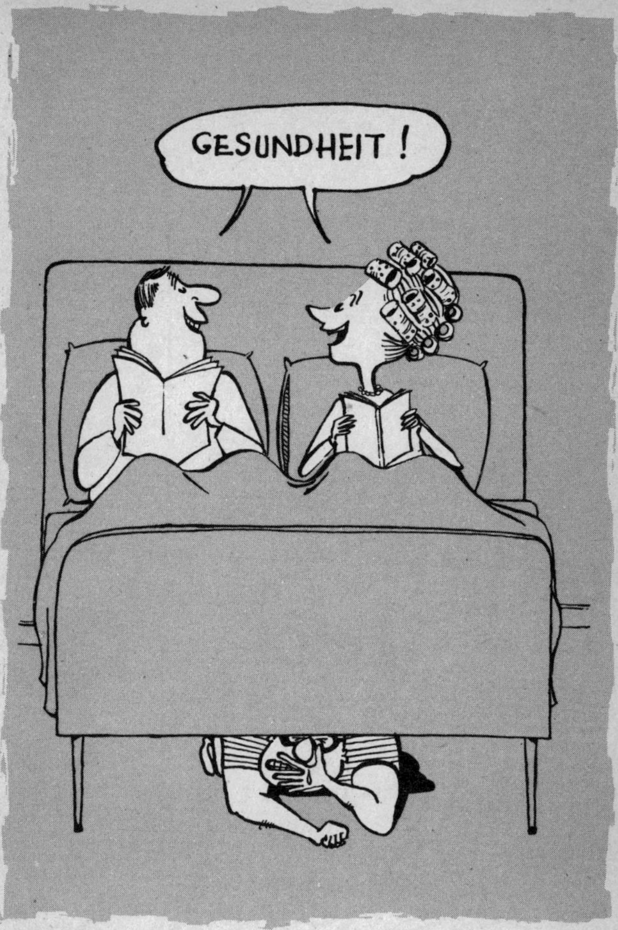
GESUNDHEIT !

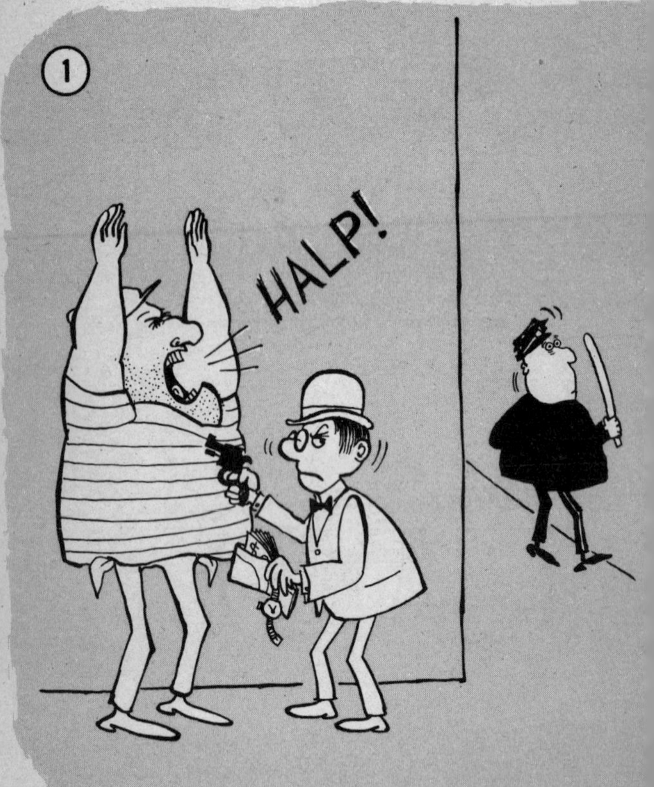
1
HALP!

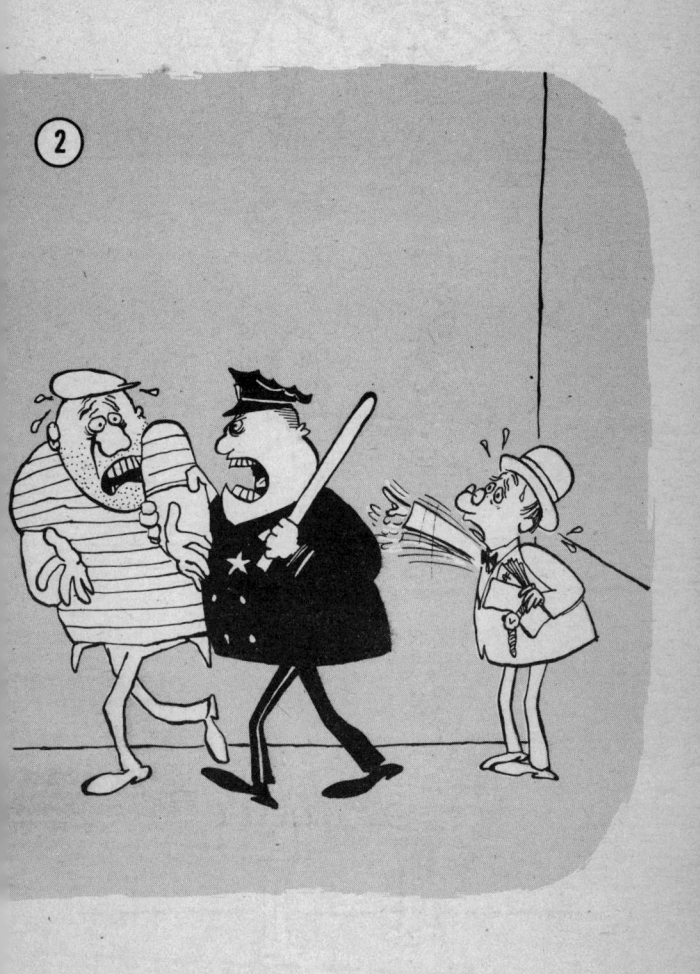

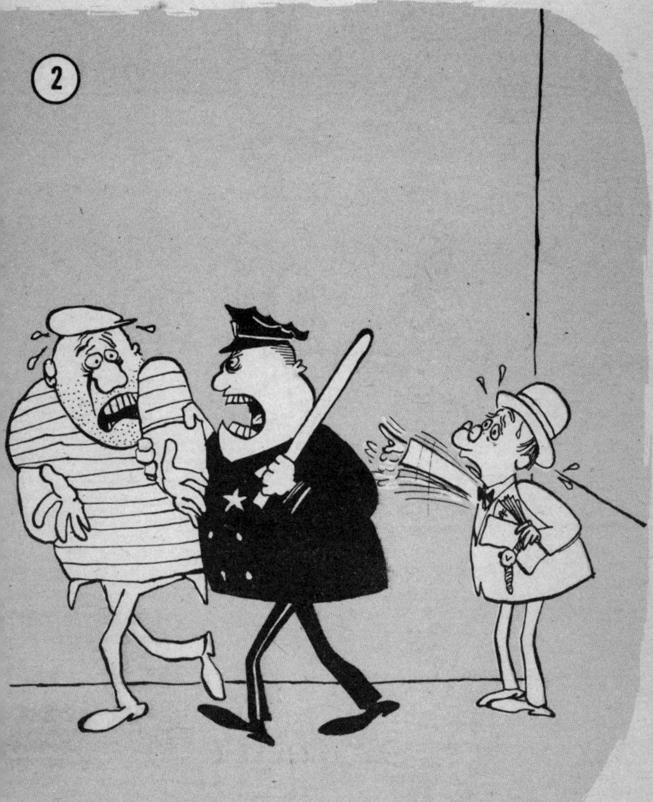
2

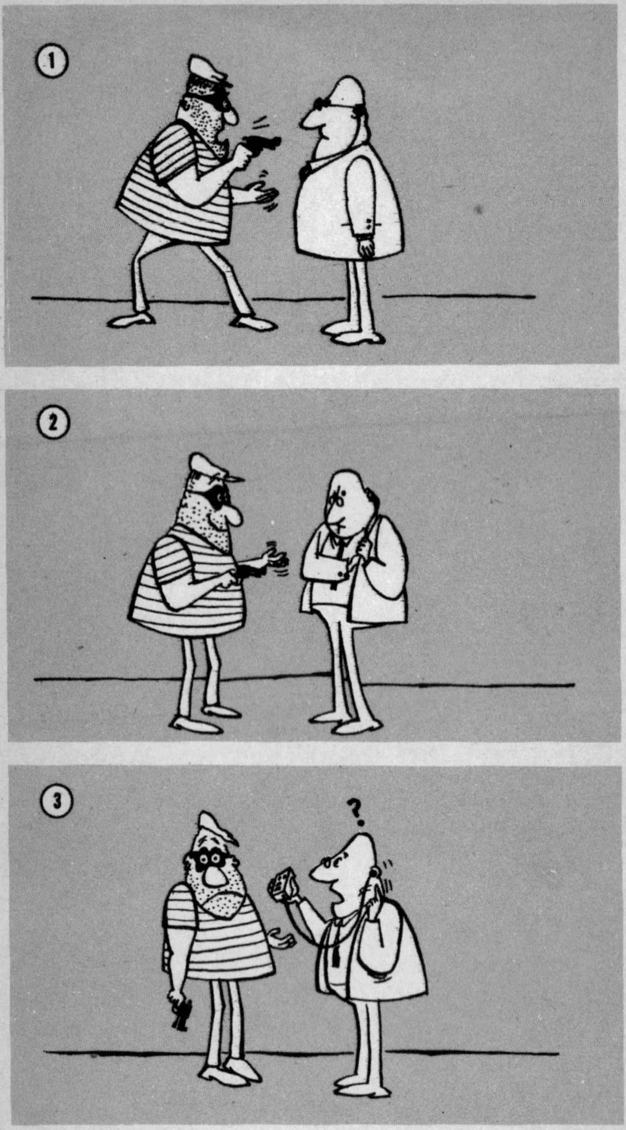
1
2
3
?

VIVA HOSPITALS!

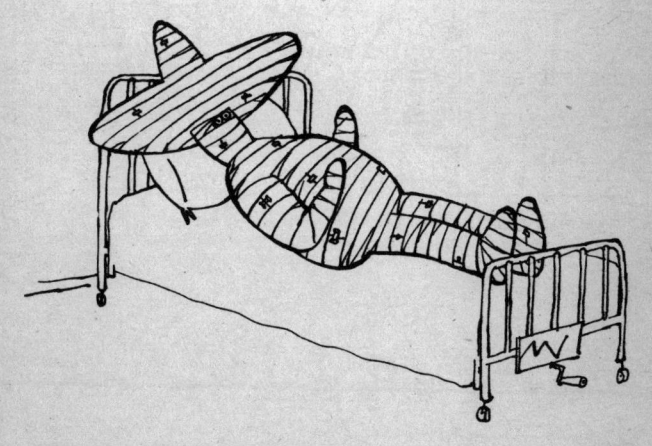

(1)

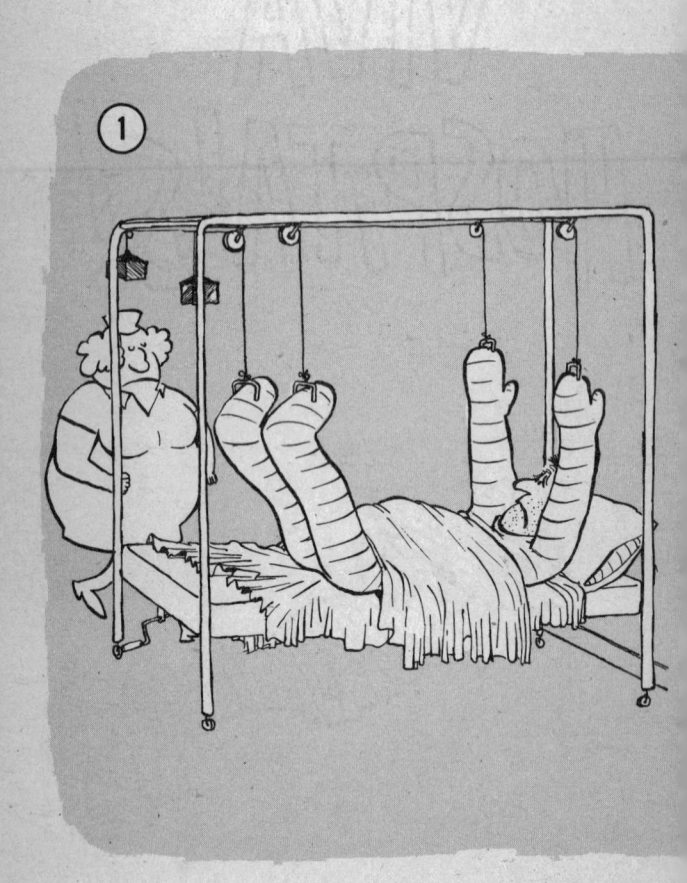

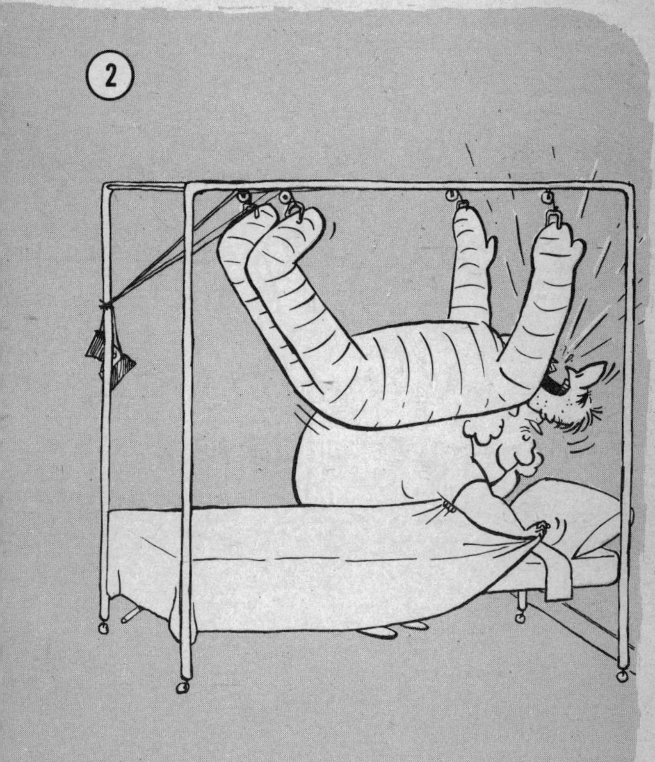
2

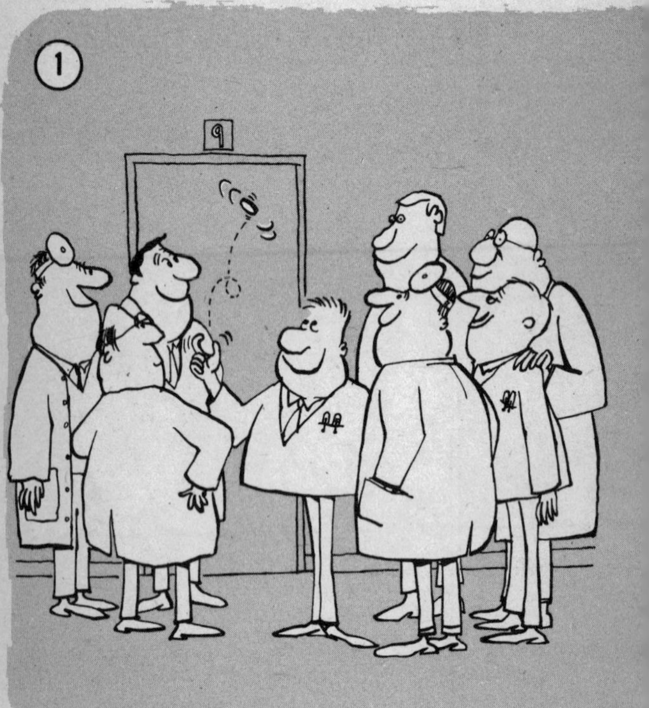
1
9

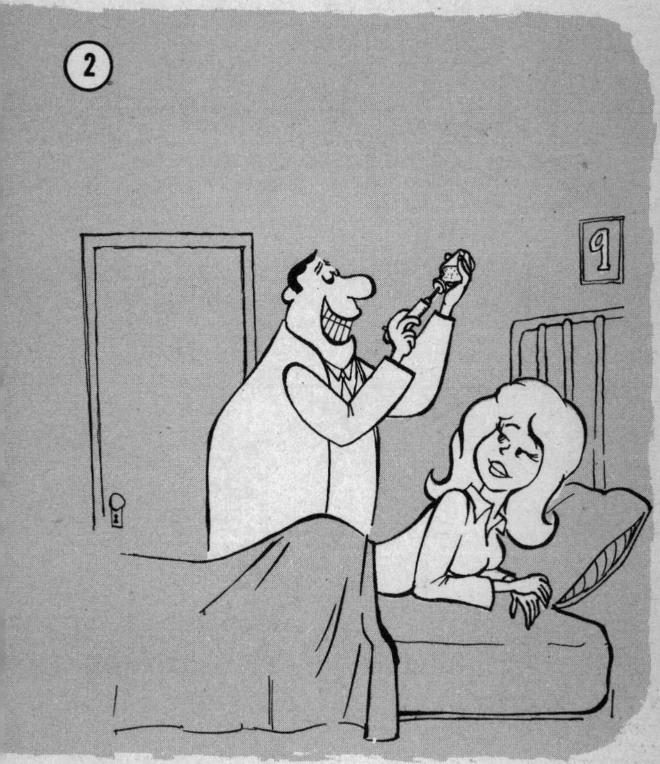
2
9

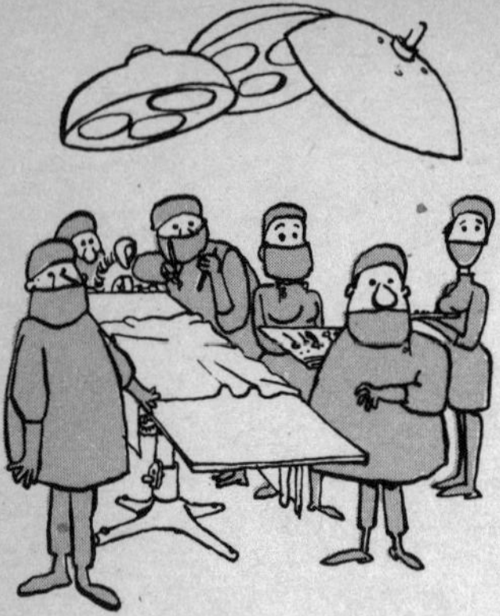

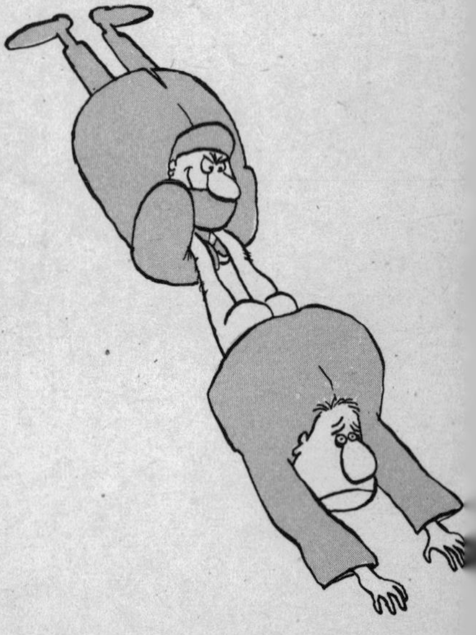

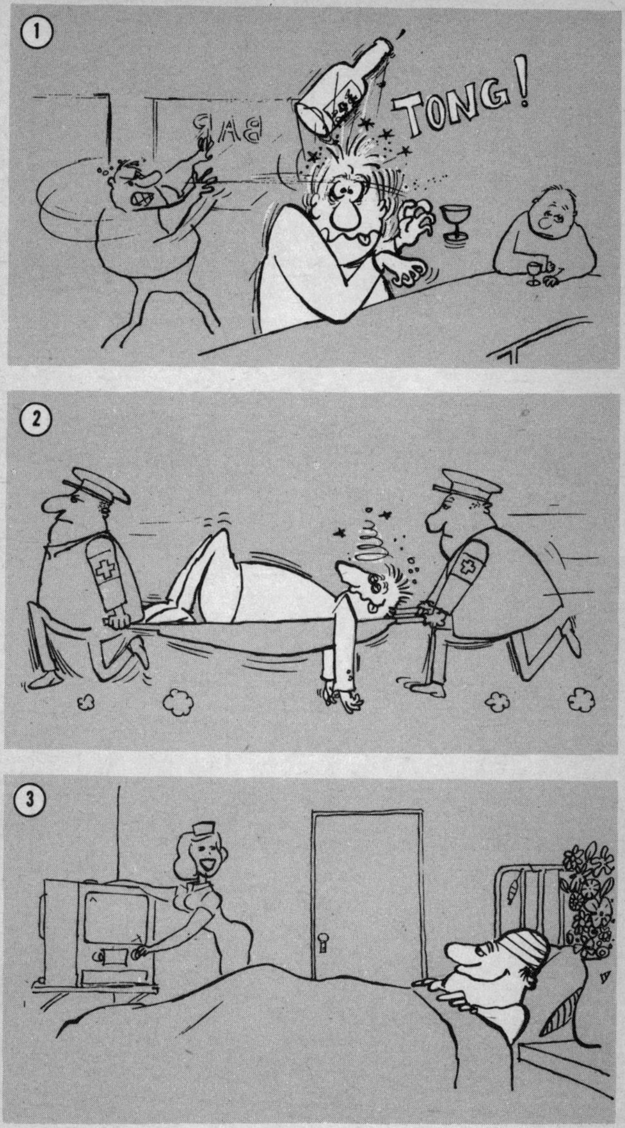
1
TONG!
2
3

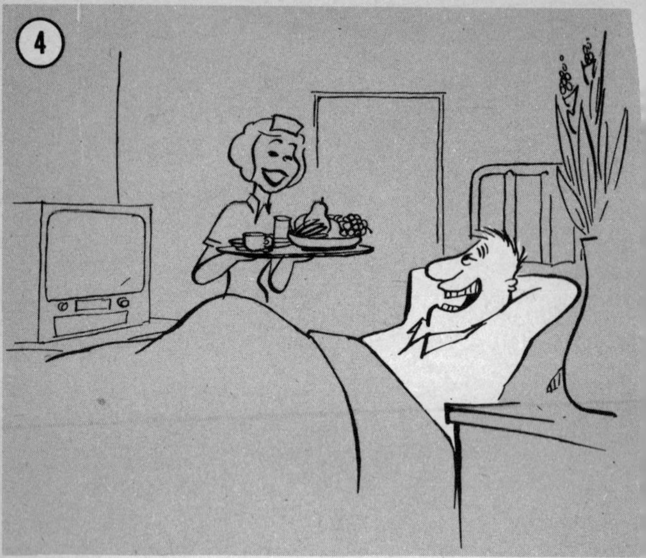
4

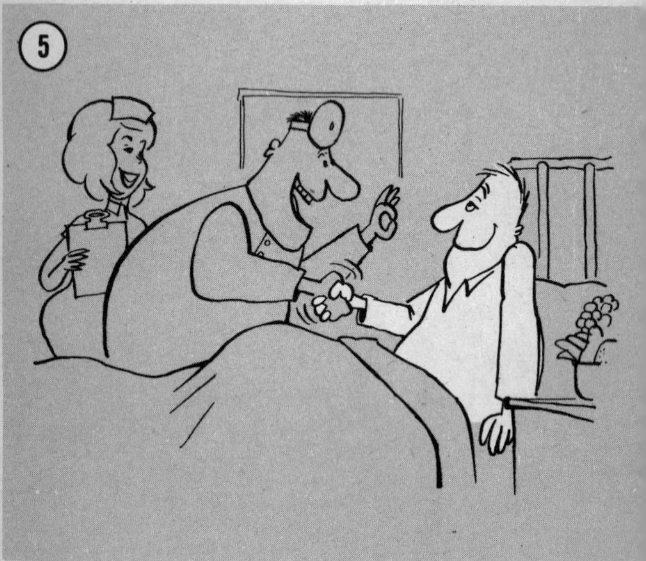
5

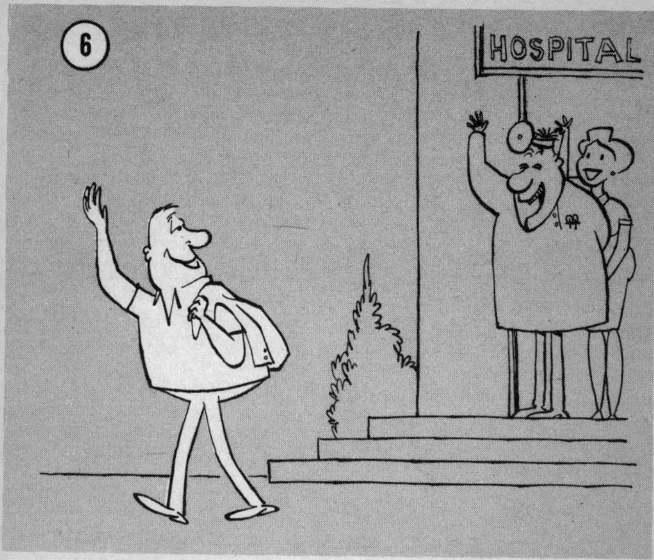
6
HOSPITAL

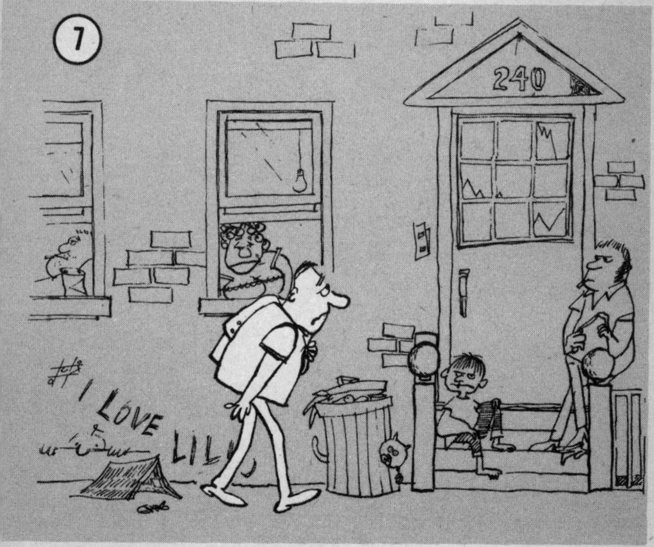
7
240
I LOVE
LIL

(8)

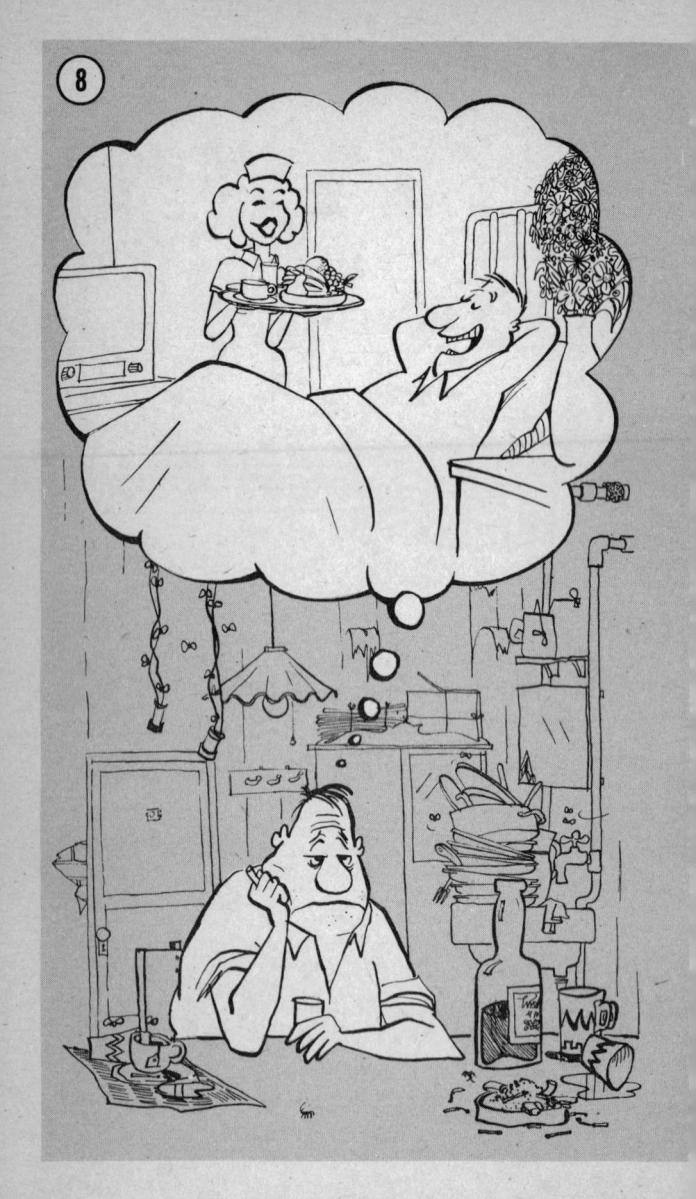

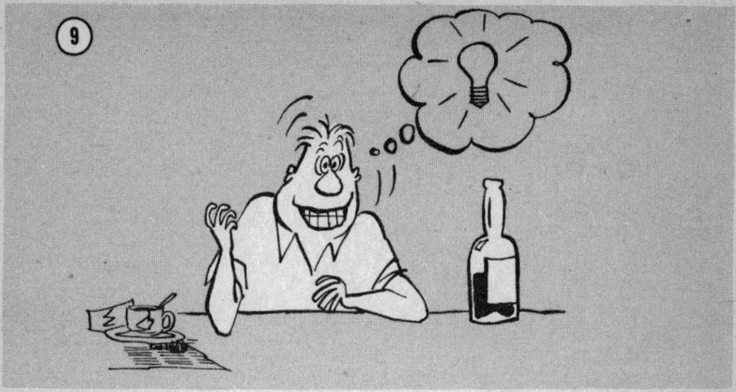
9

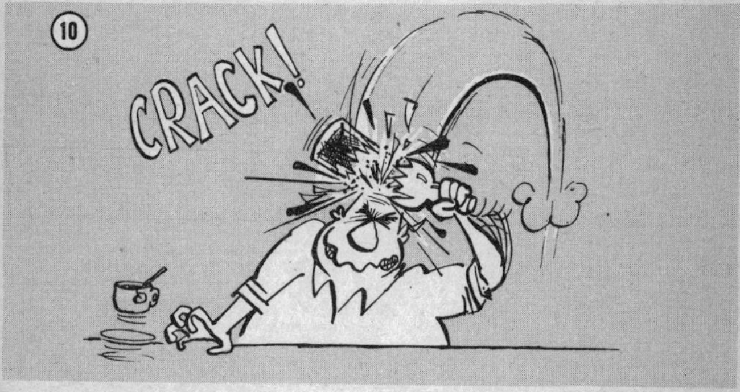
10
CRACK!

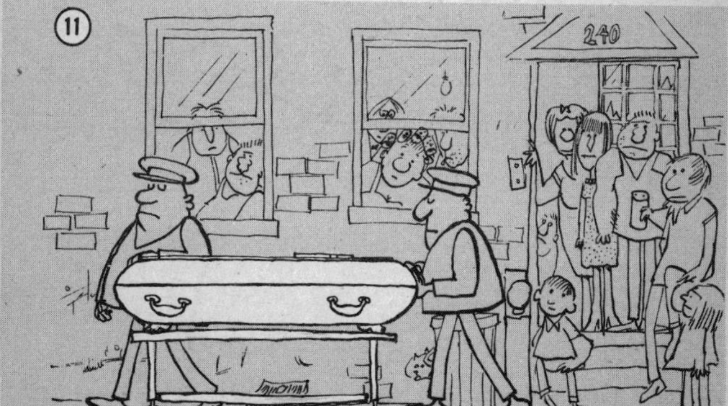
11
240

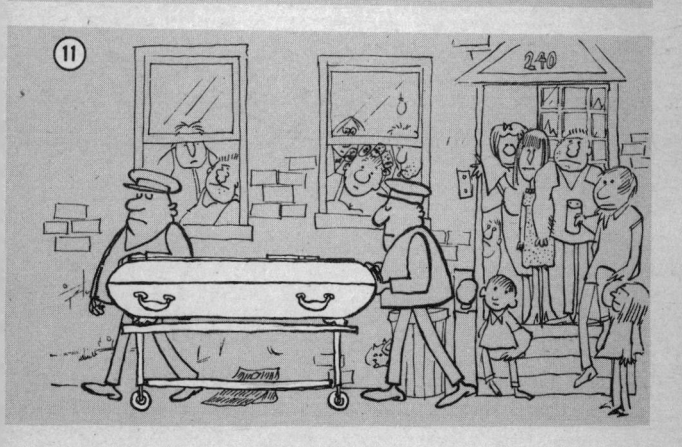

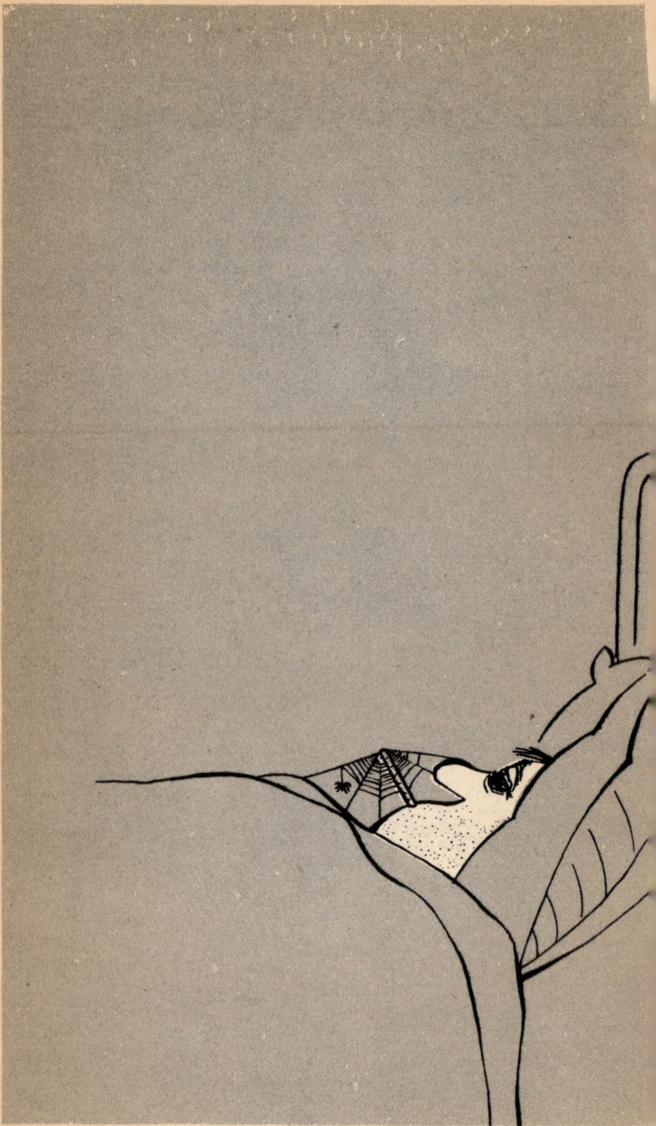

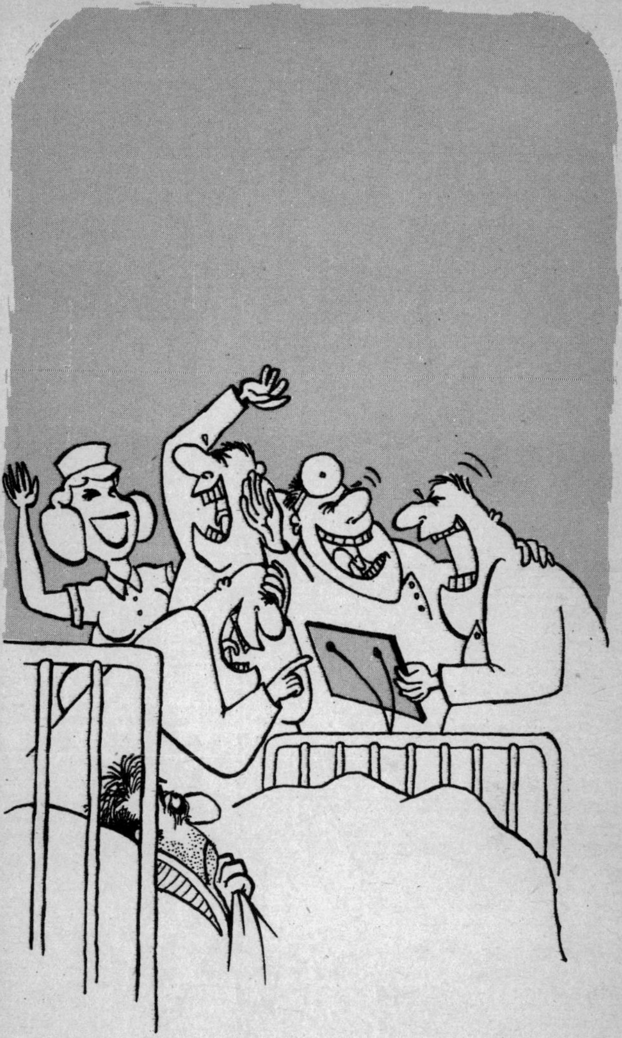

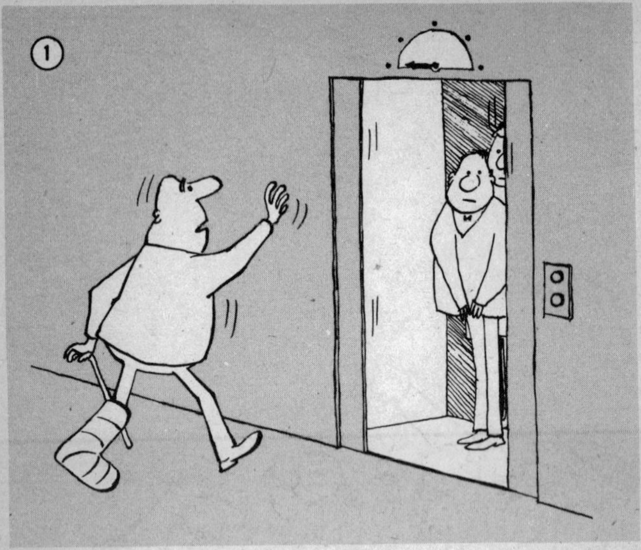

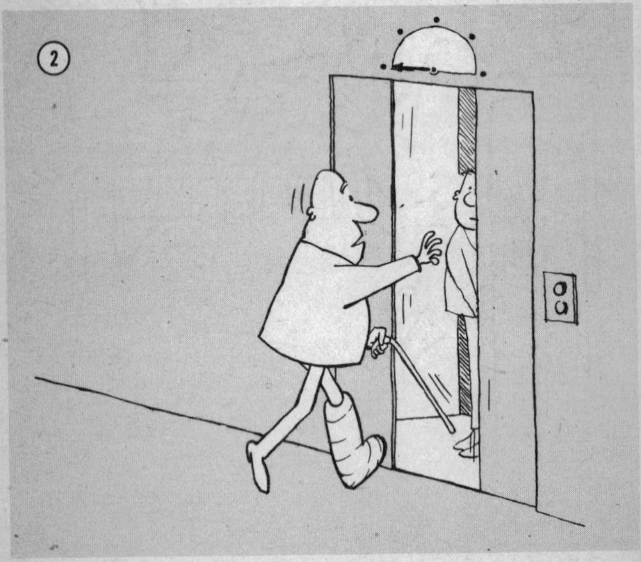

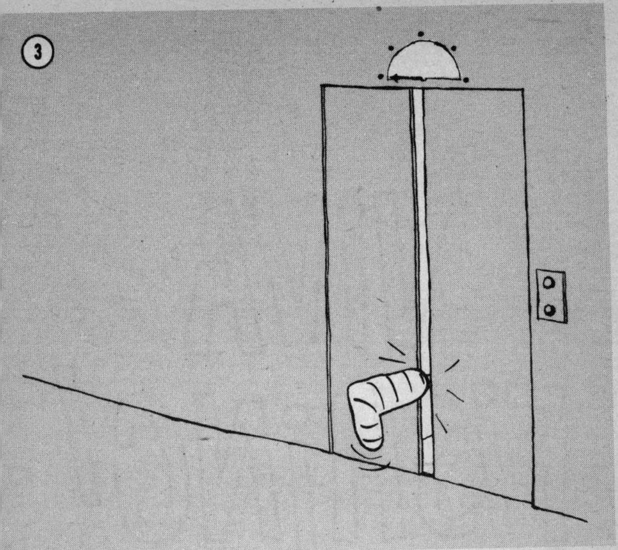
3

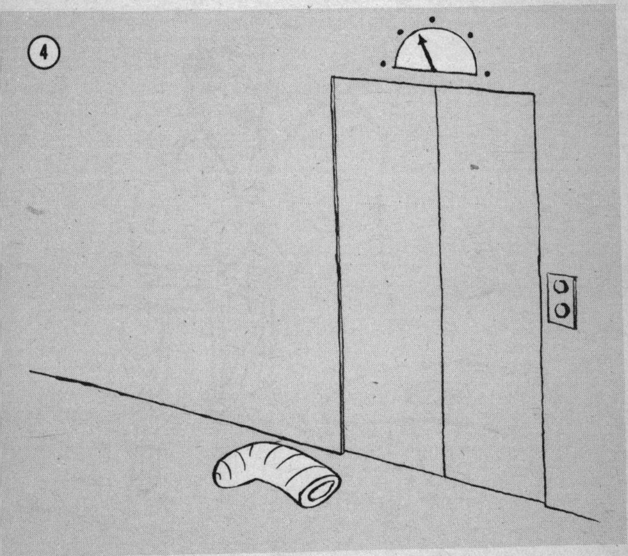
4

VIVA FISHING!

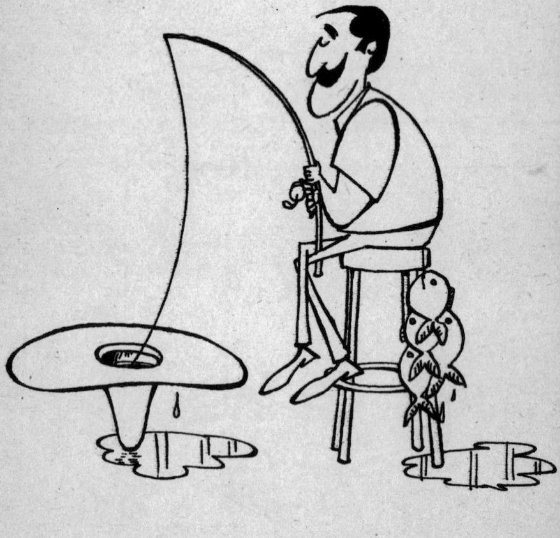

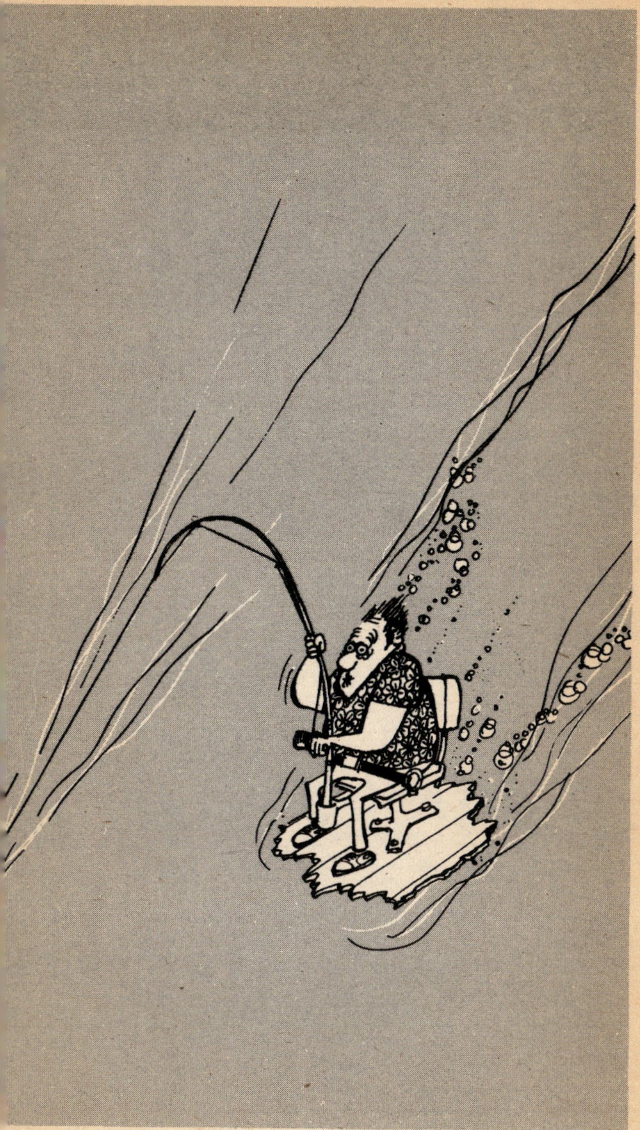

116

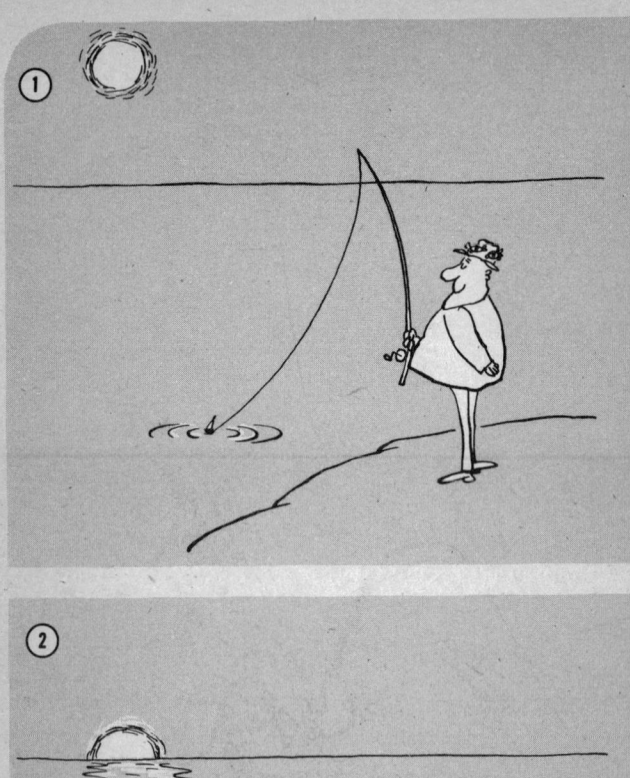

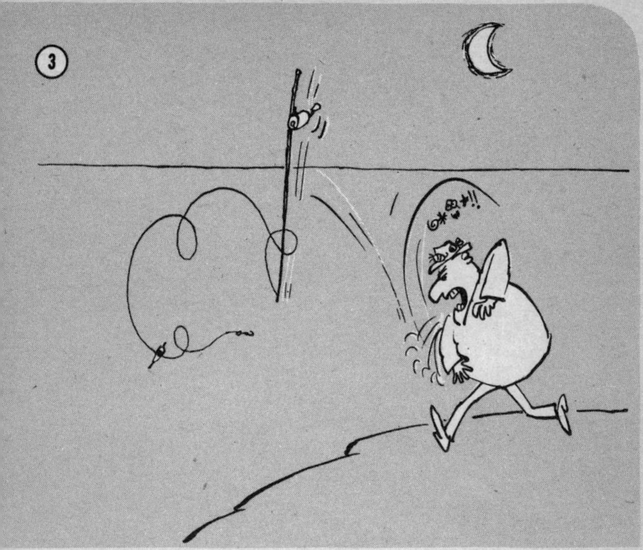
3

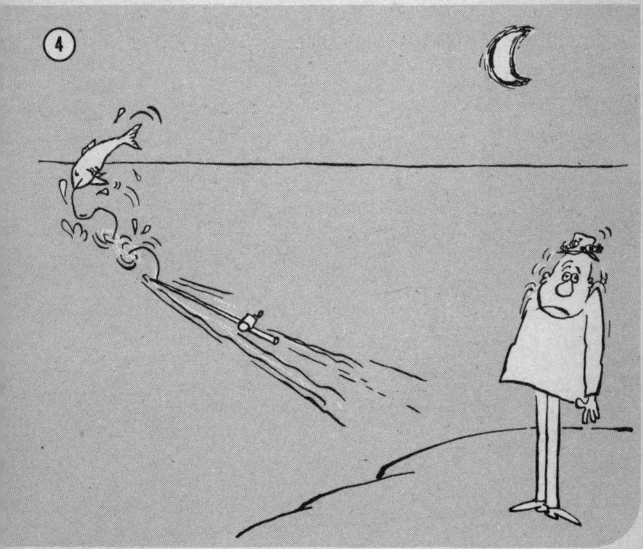
4

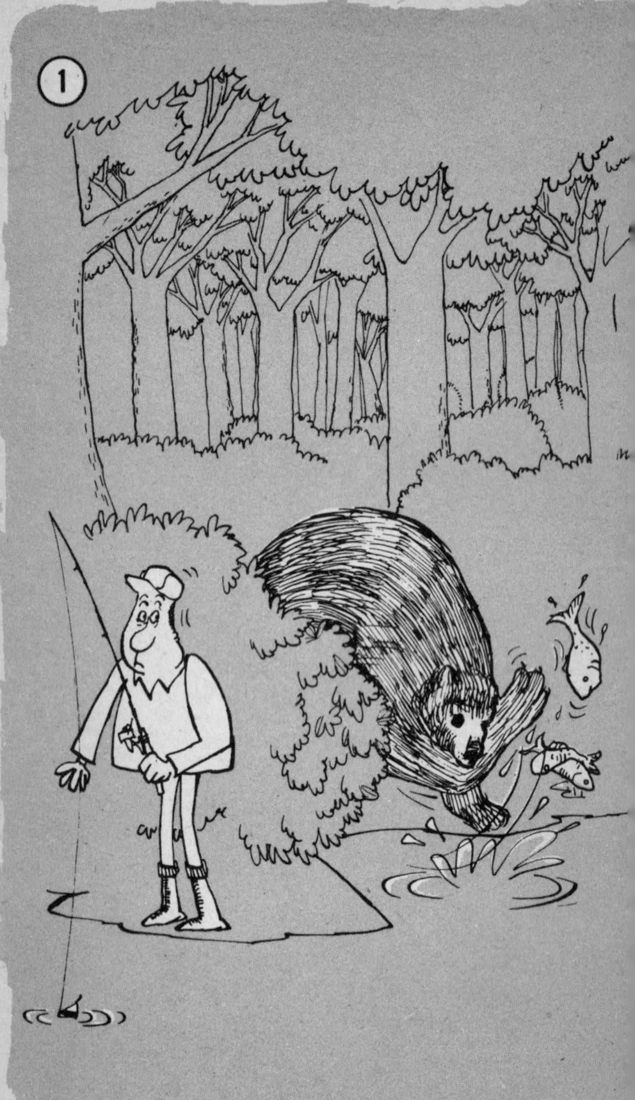
1

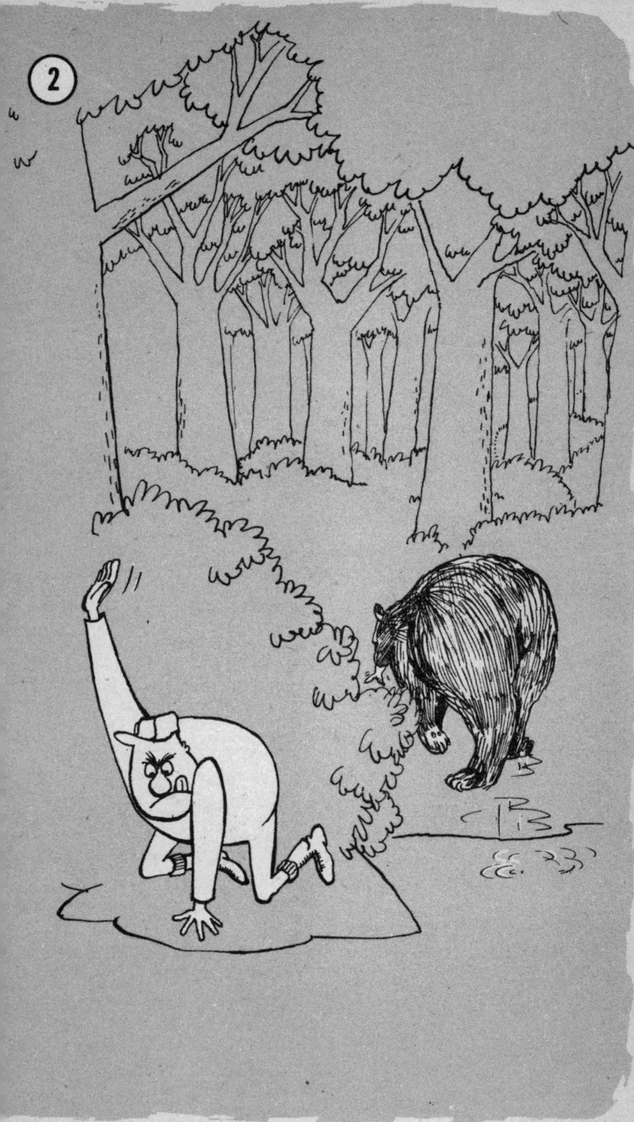

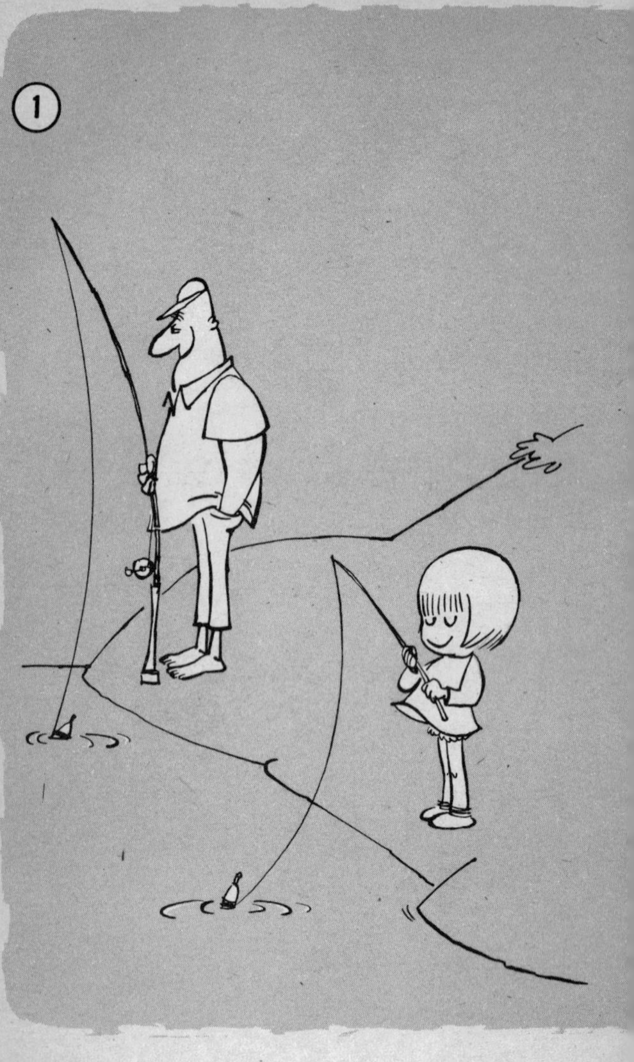
1

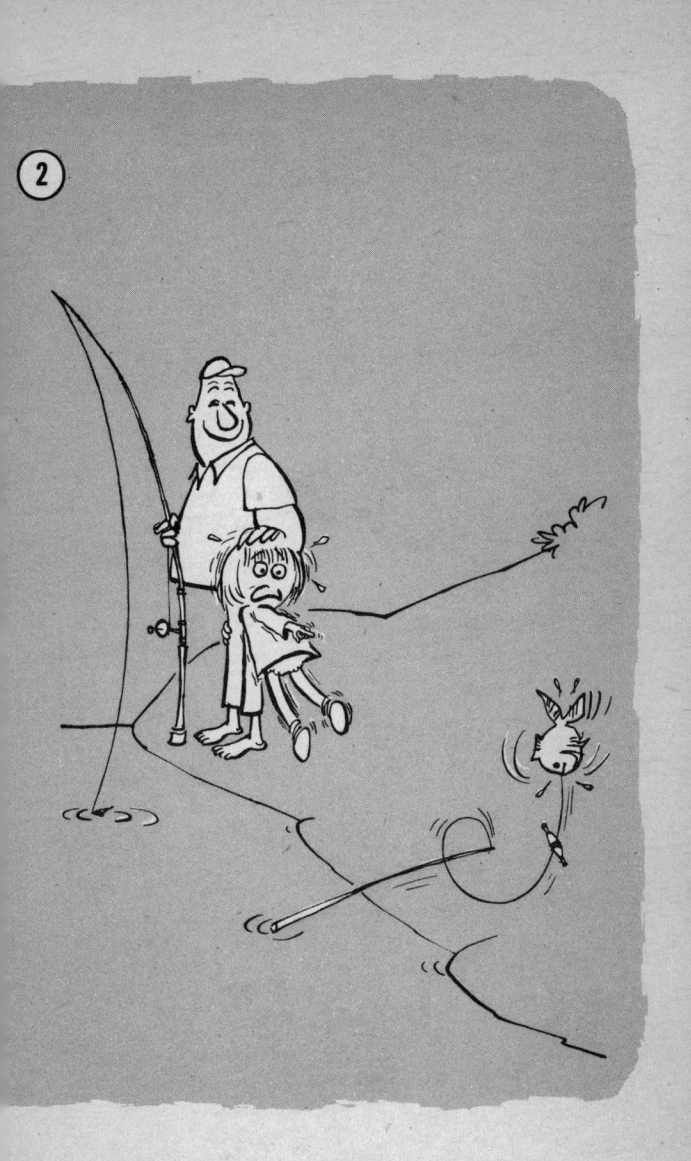

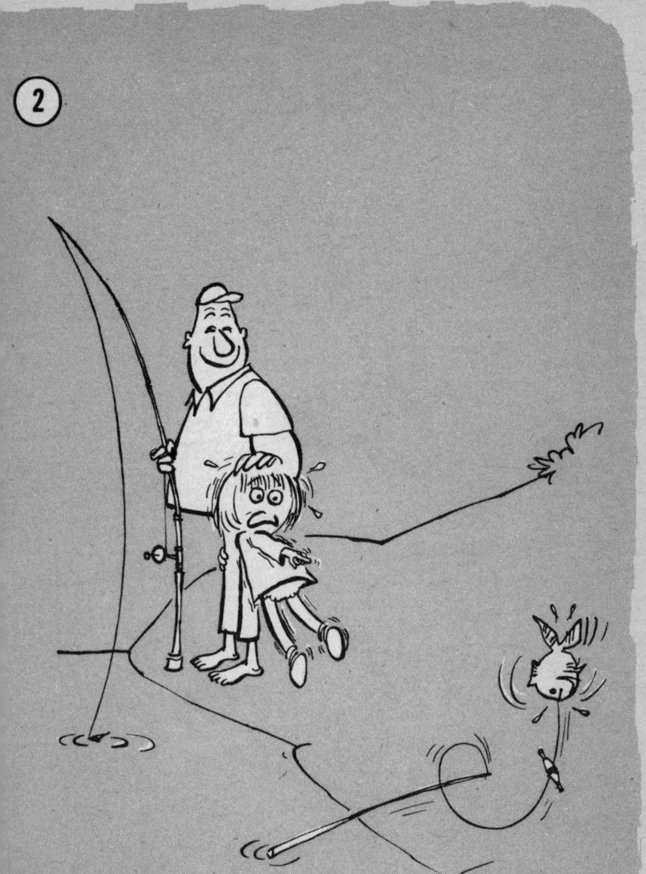
2

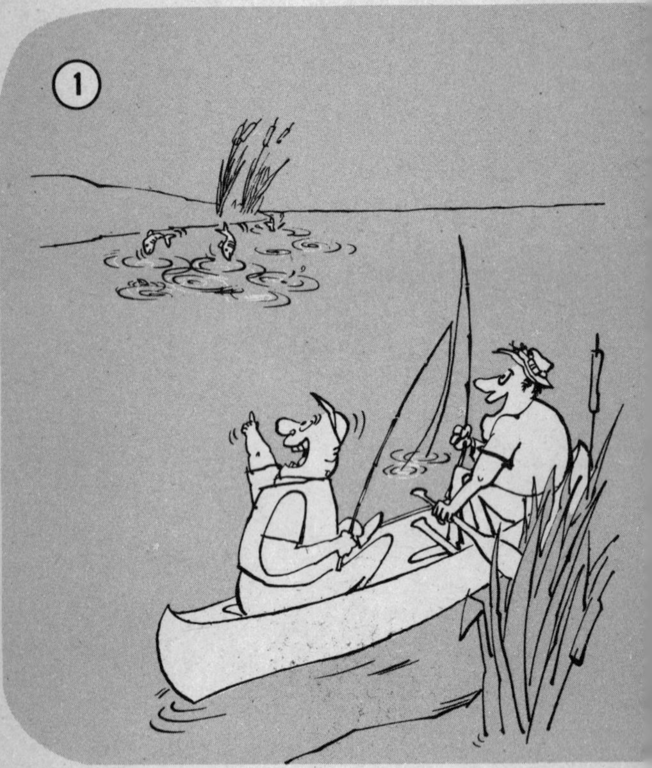
1

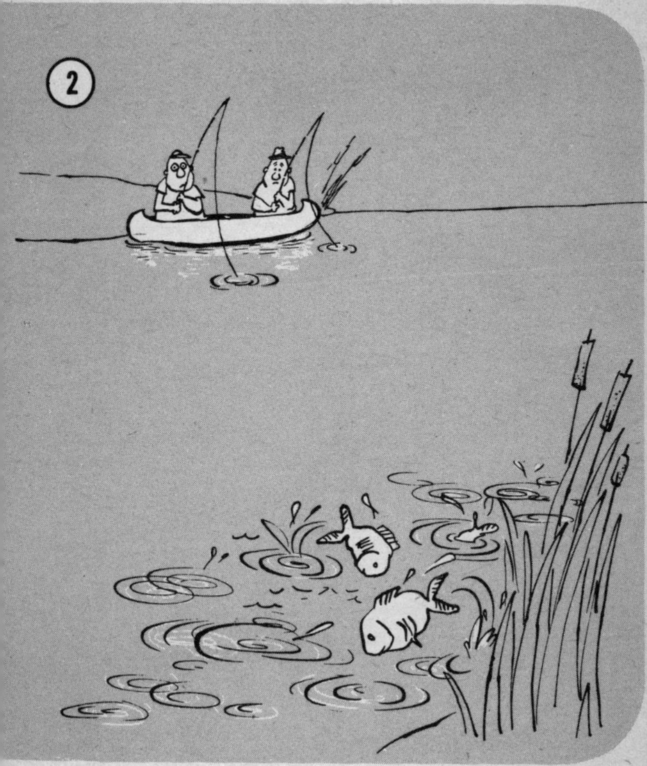
2

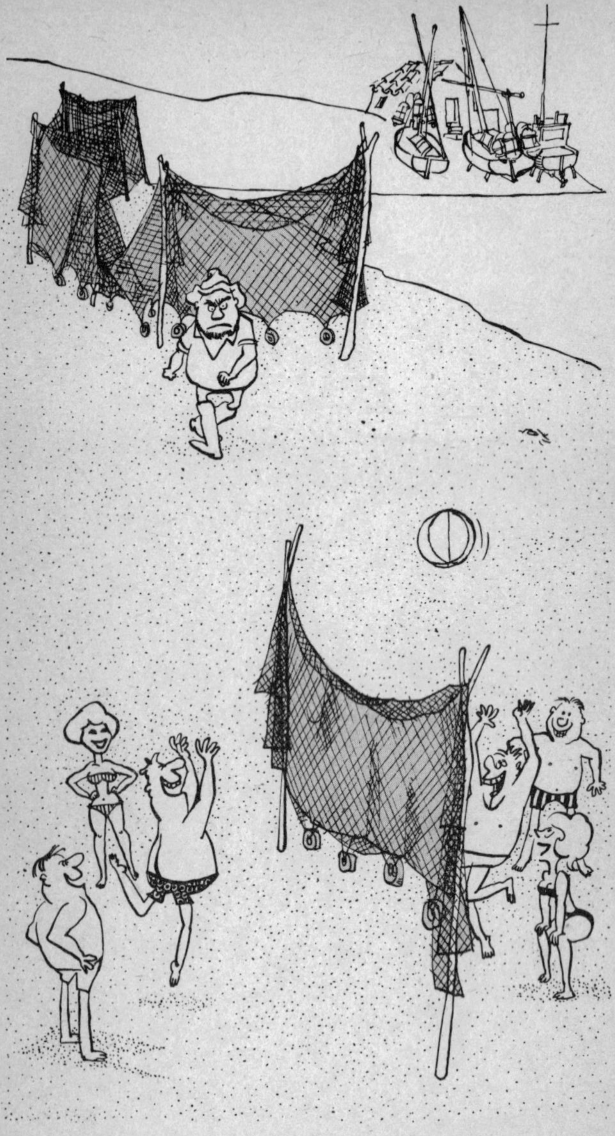

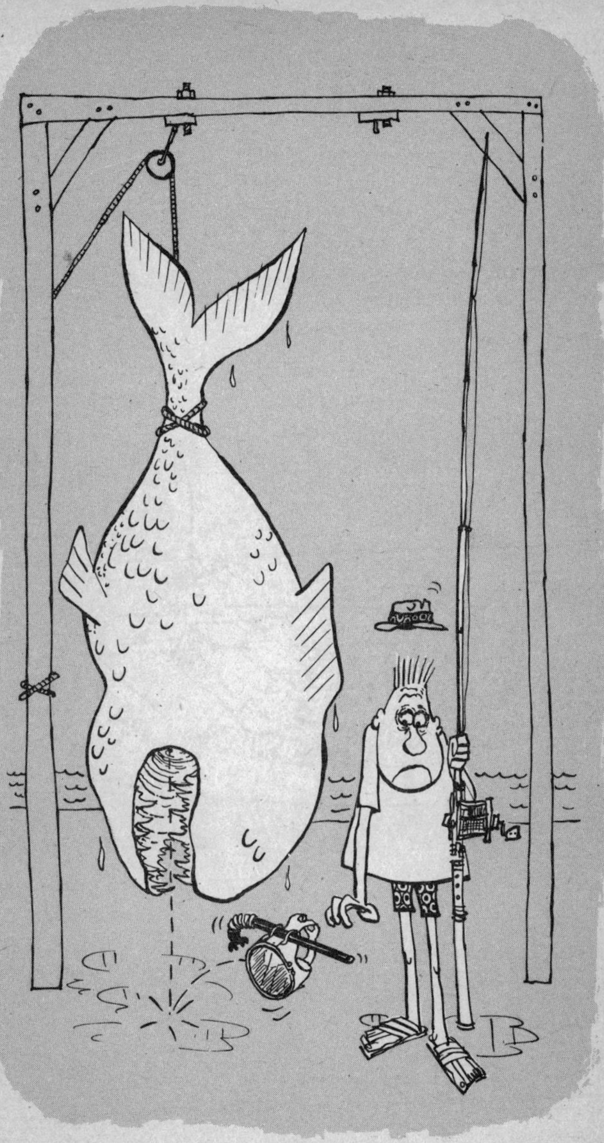

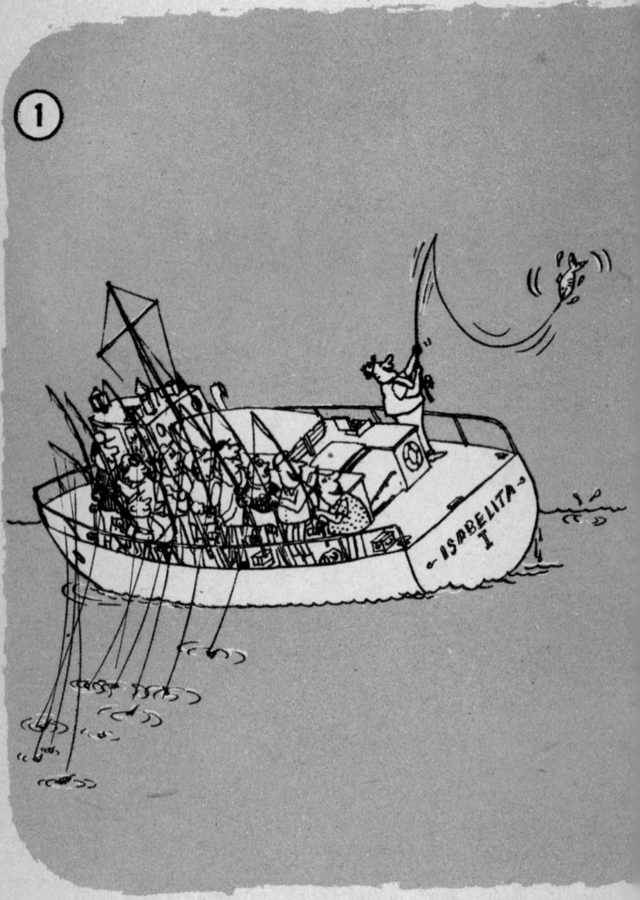
1
ISABELITA
I

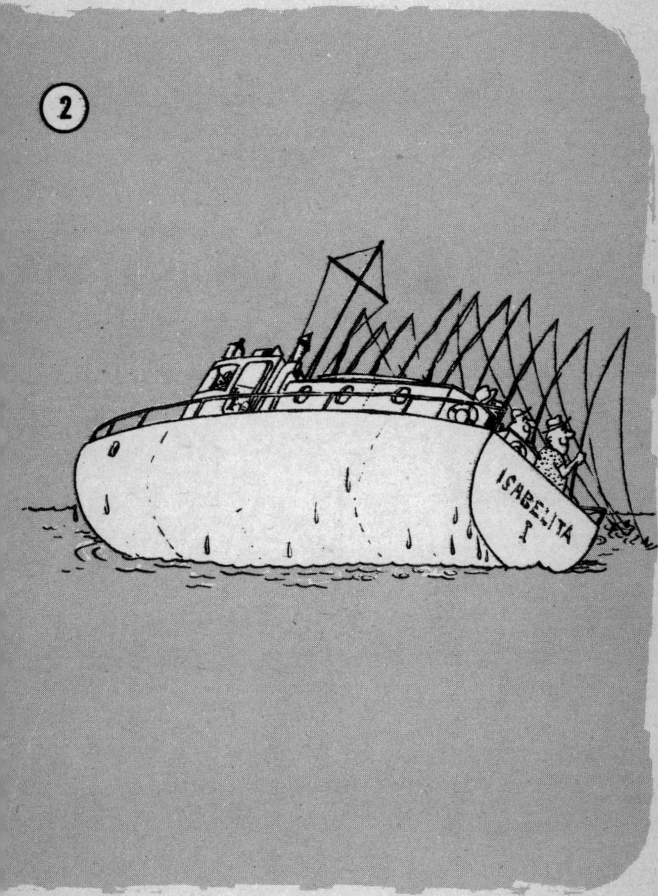
2
ISABELITA
I

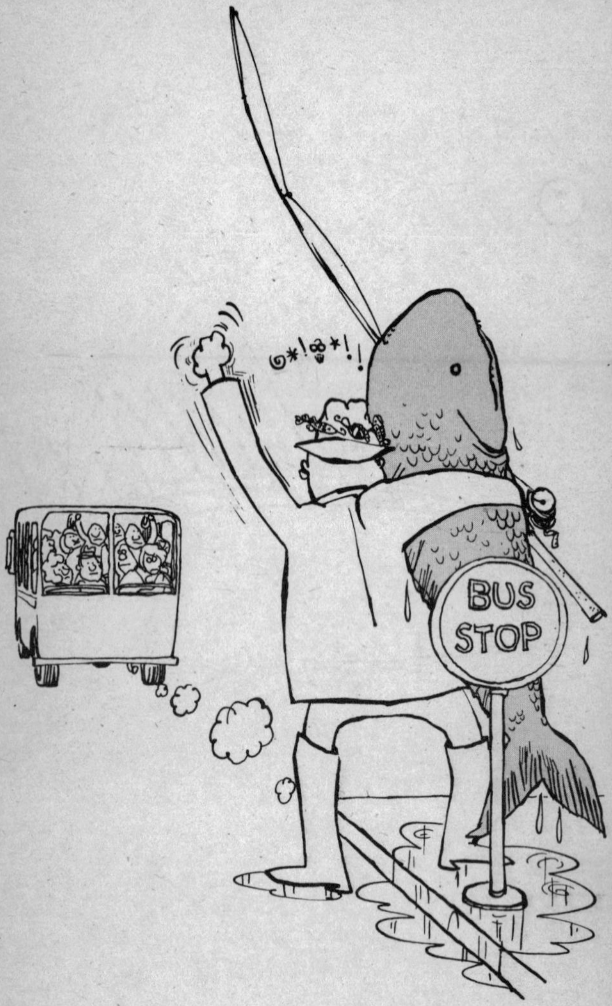
BUS
STOP

VIVA WINTER!

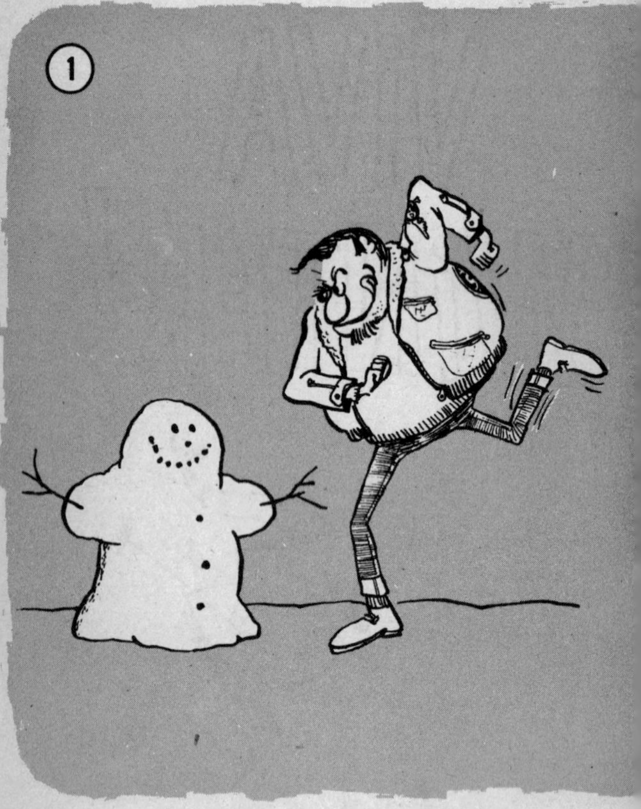
1

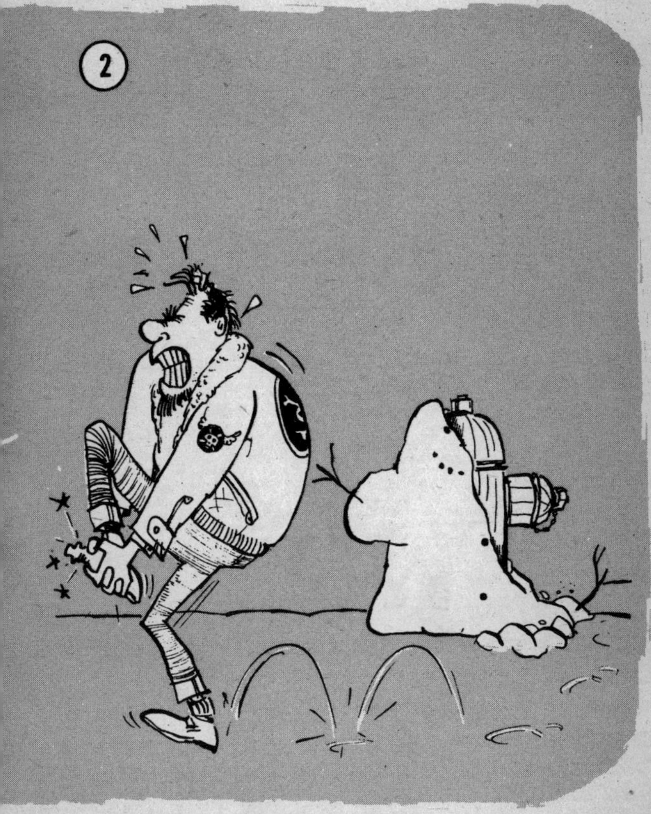
2

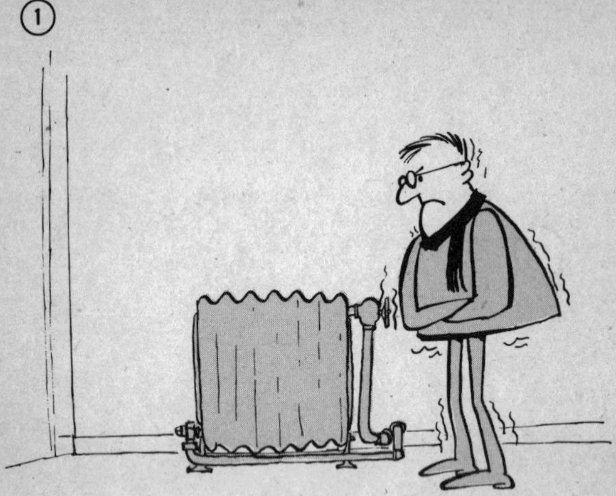

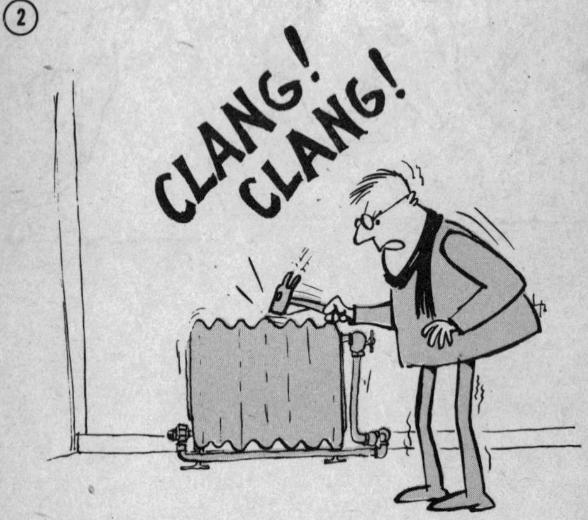
CLANG!
CLANG!

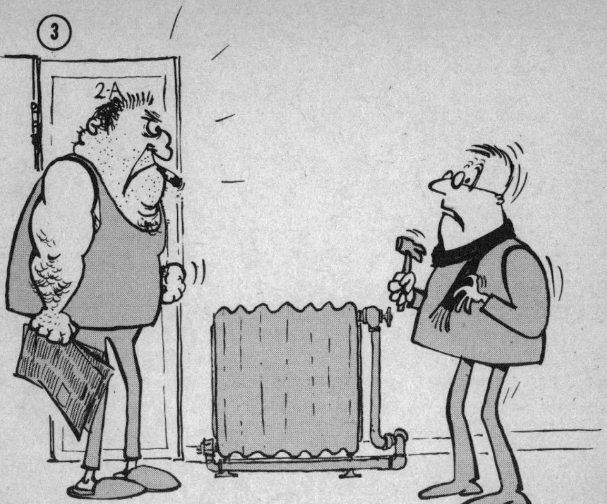
3
2-A

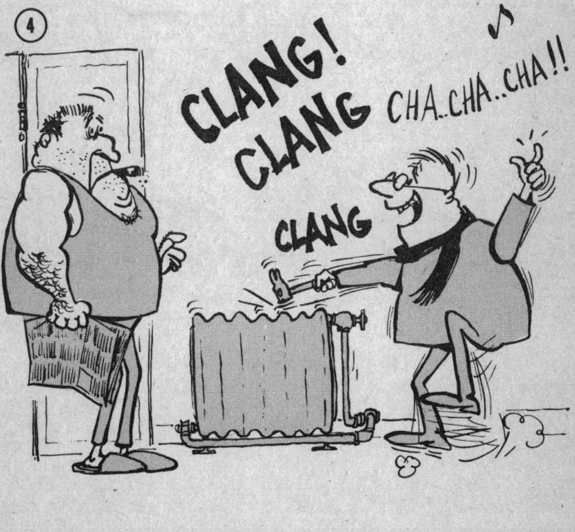
4
CLANG!
CLANG
CHA..CHA..CHA!!
CLANG

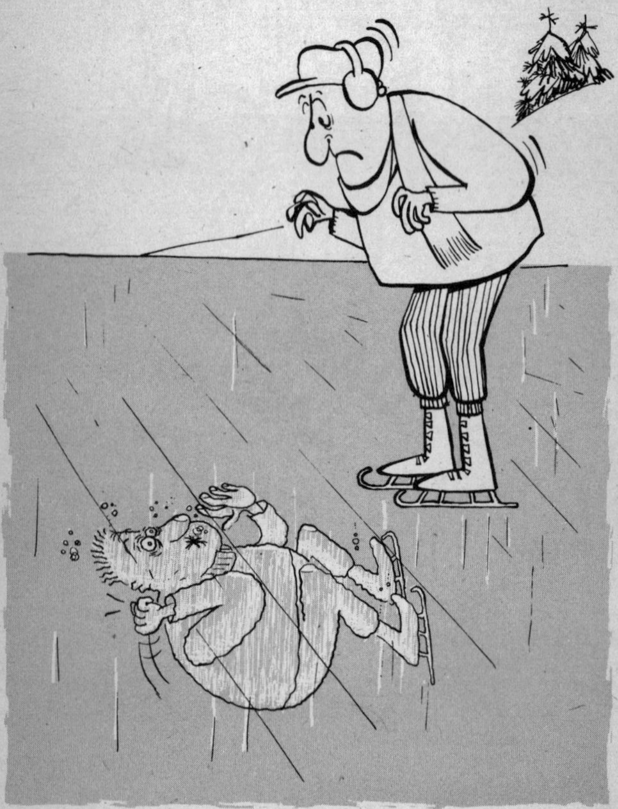

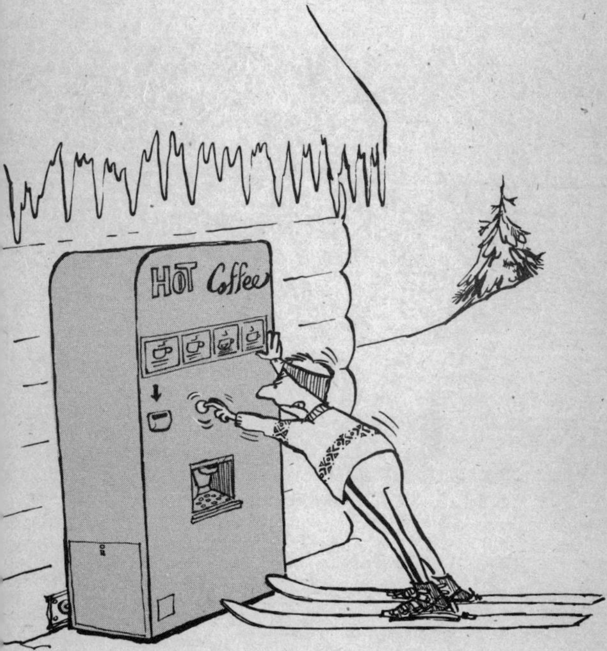
HOT Coffee

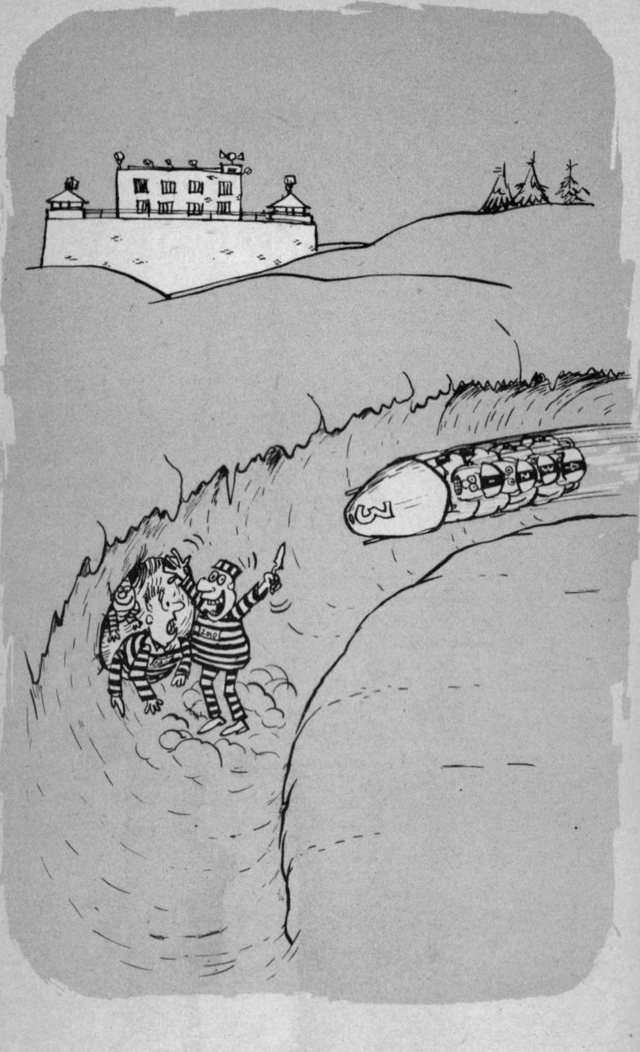

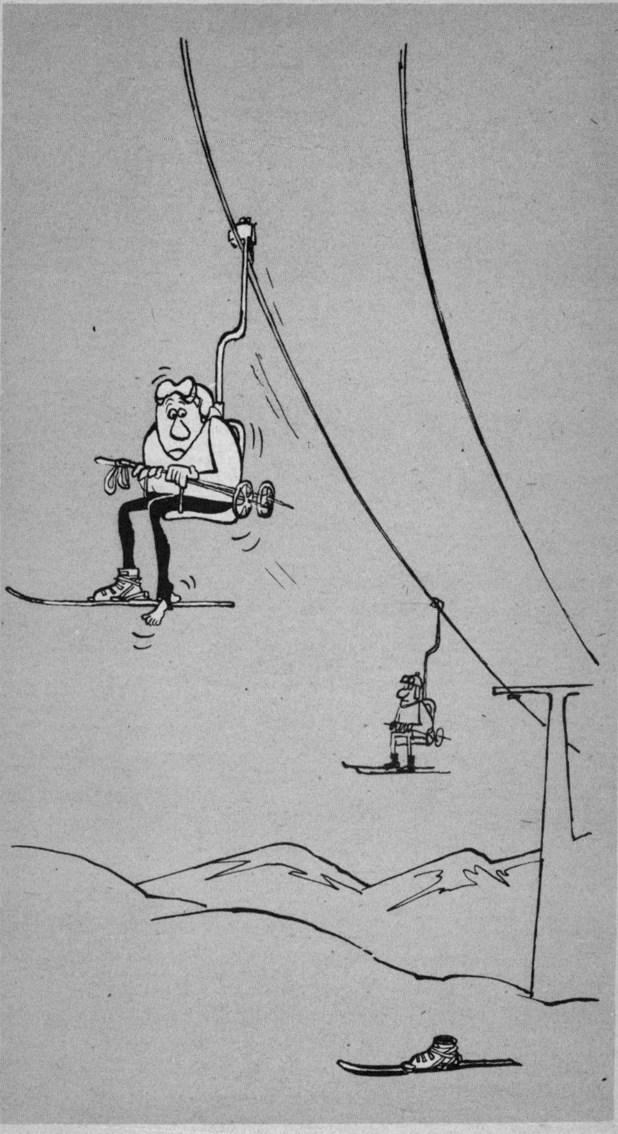

①

(2)

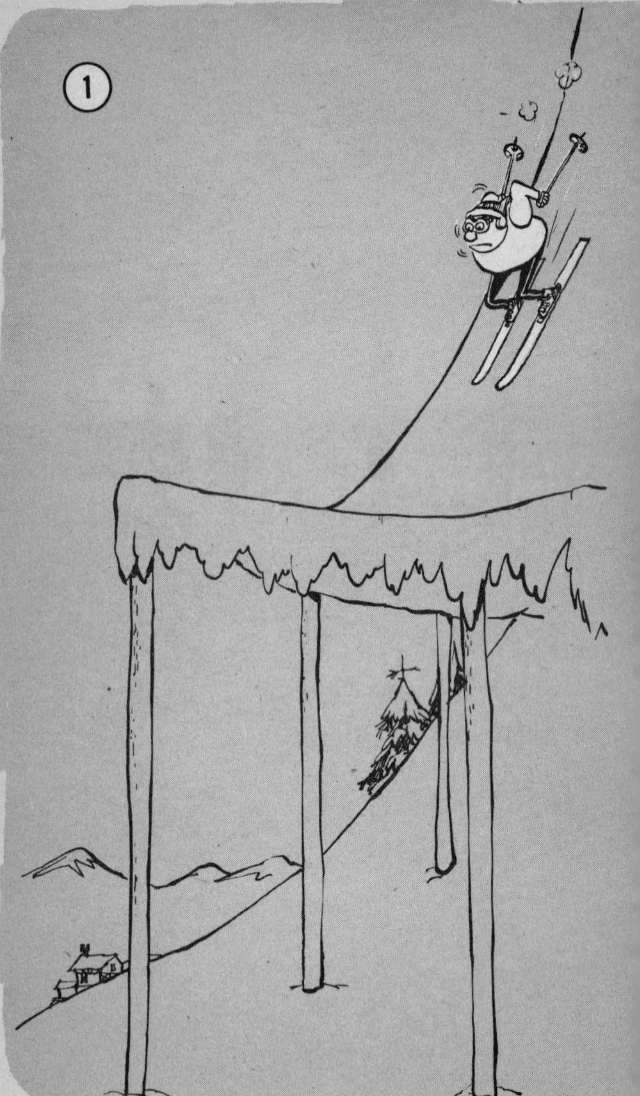
1

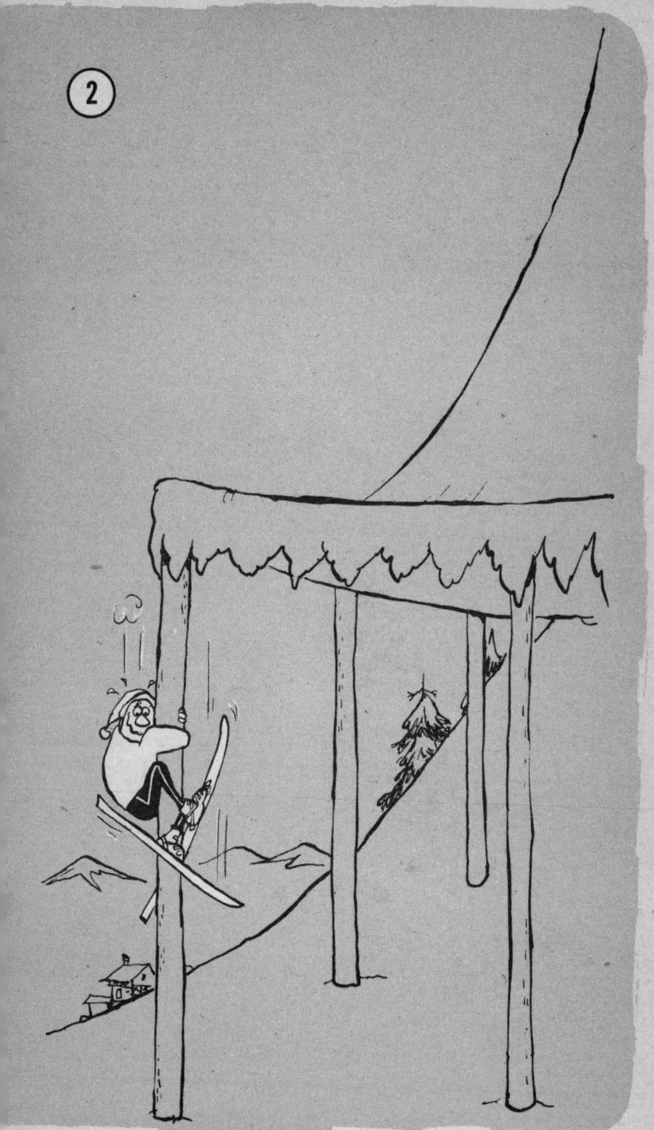
2

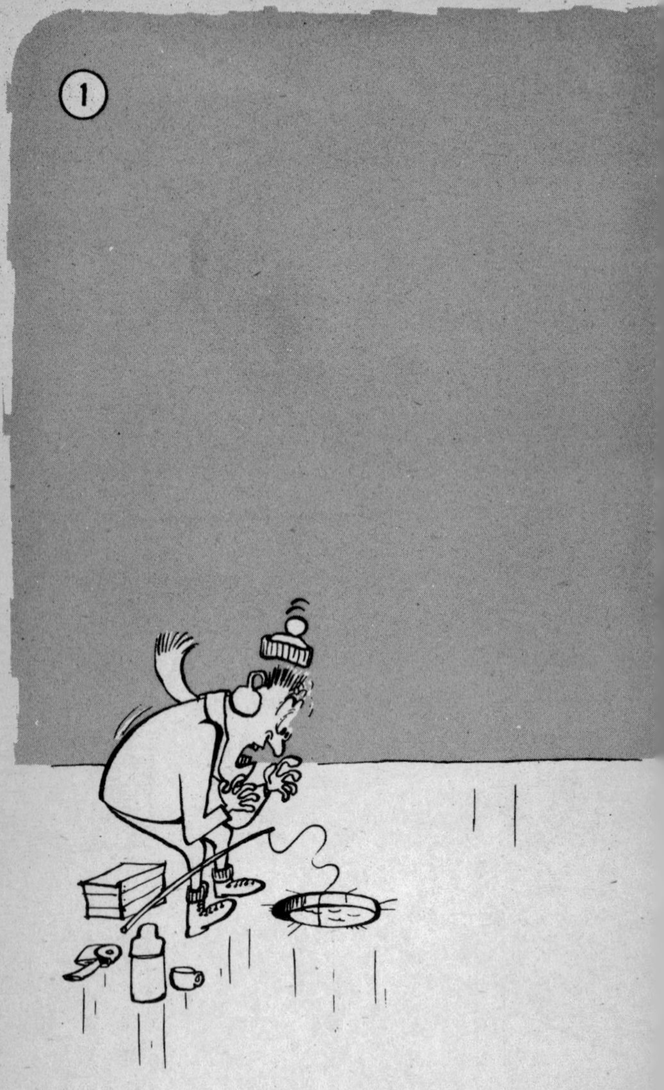
1

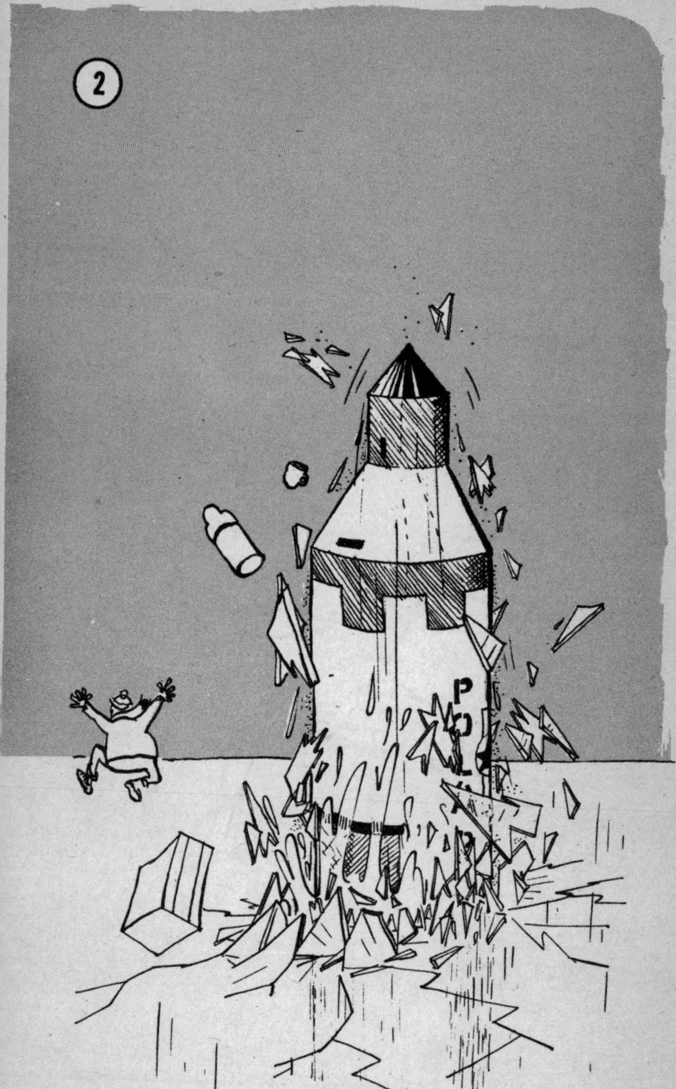
2

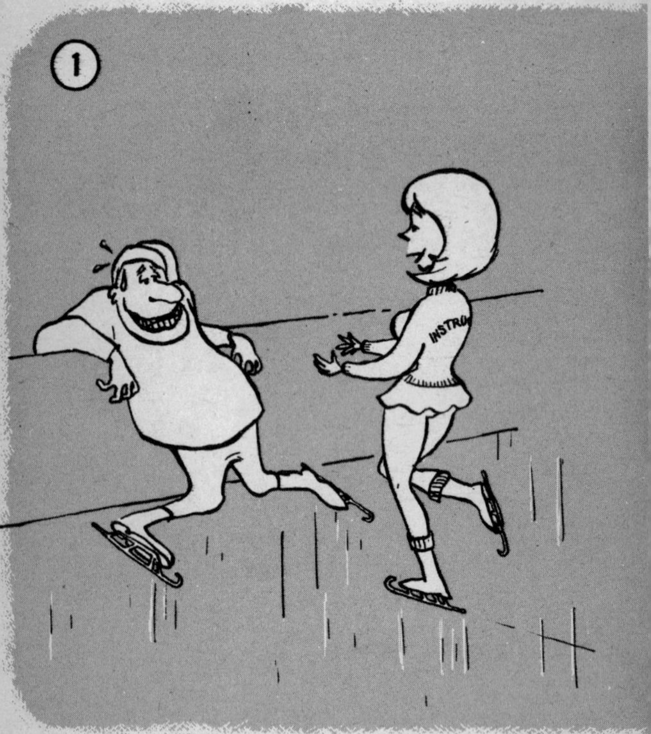
1

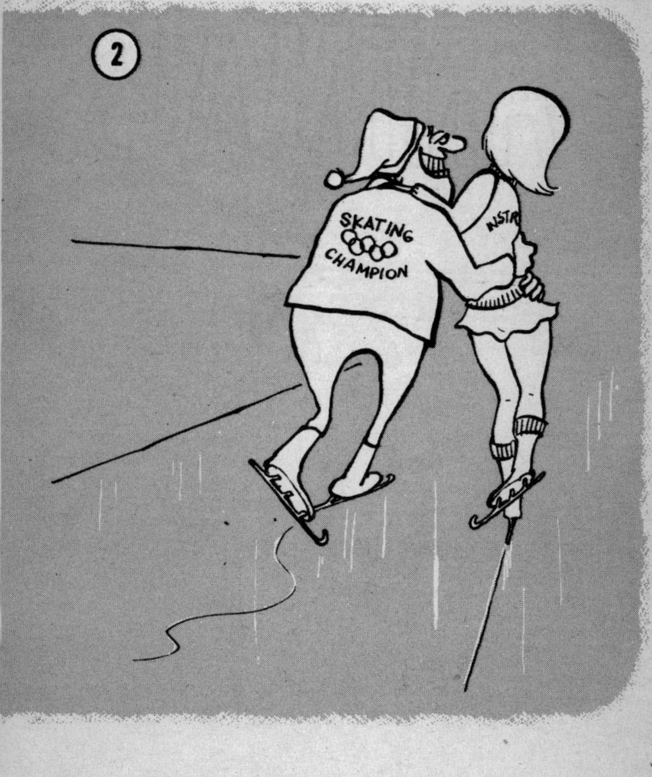
2
SKATING
CHAMPION

VIVA ANIMALS!

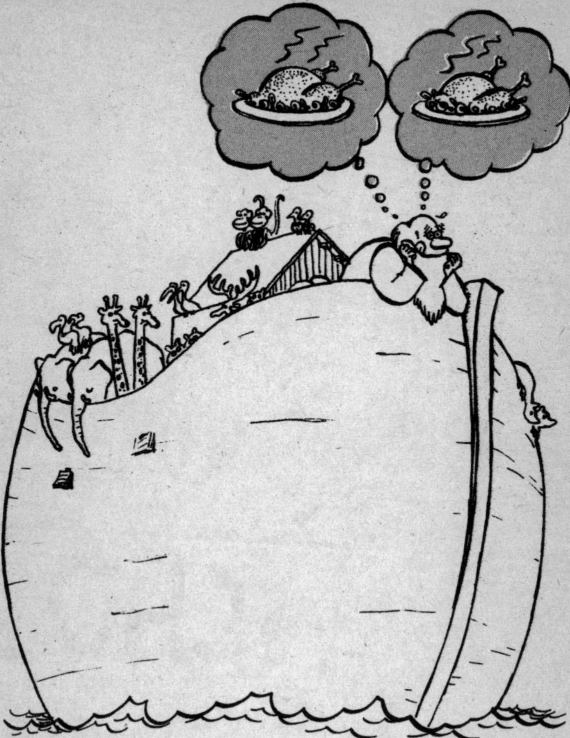

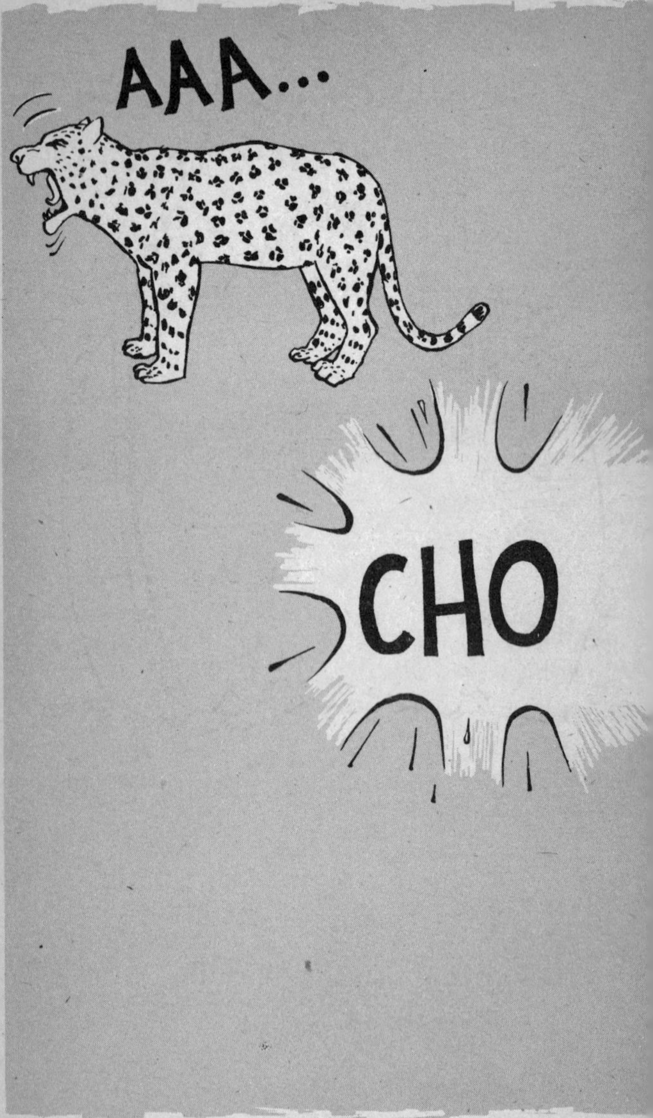
AAA...
CHO

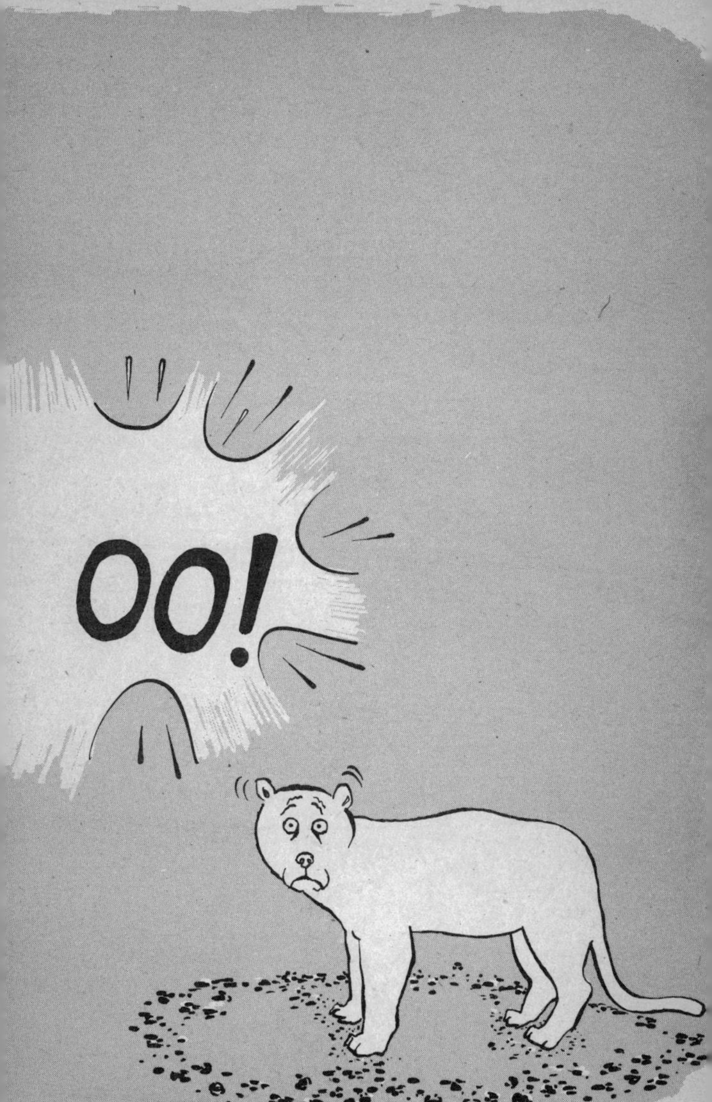
OO!

150

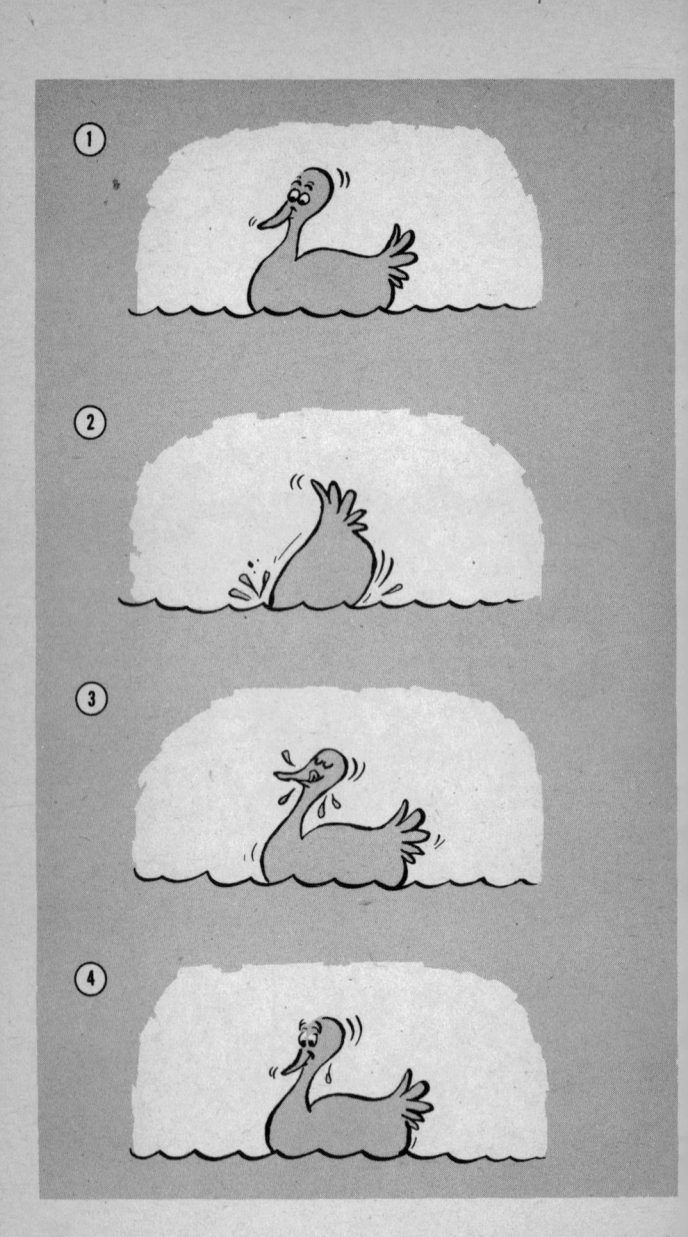

5
6
7

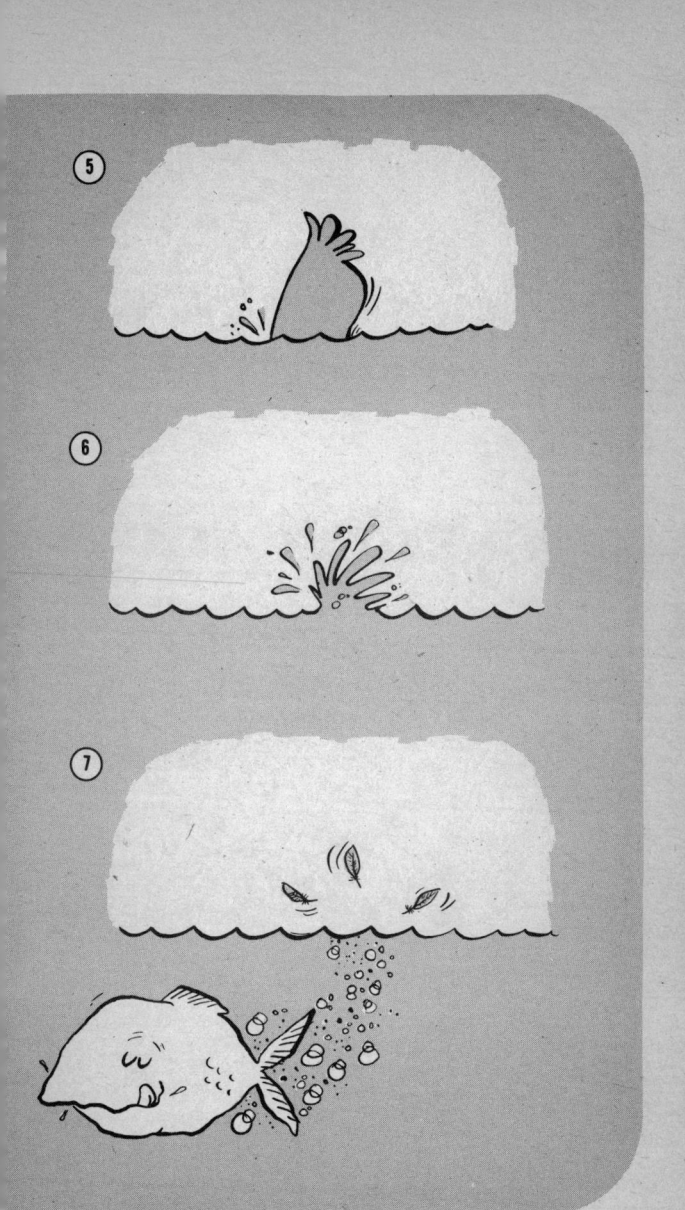

151

ALLIGATOR FARM
HSSSSS!
BEER

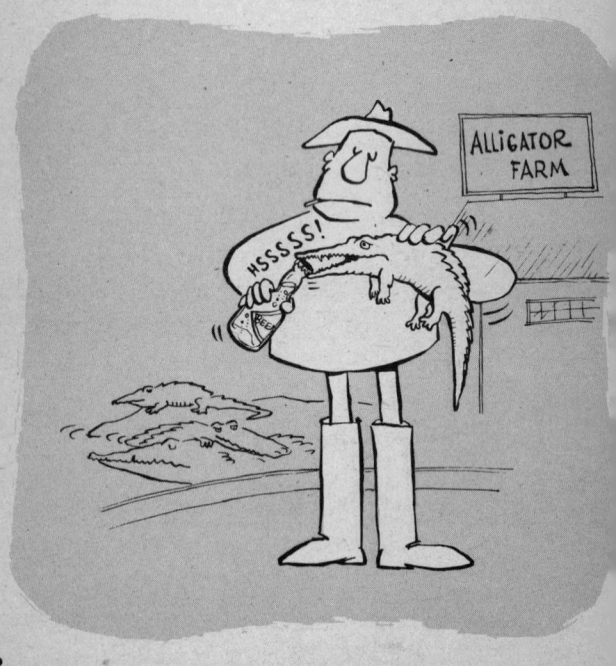

153

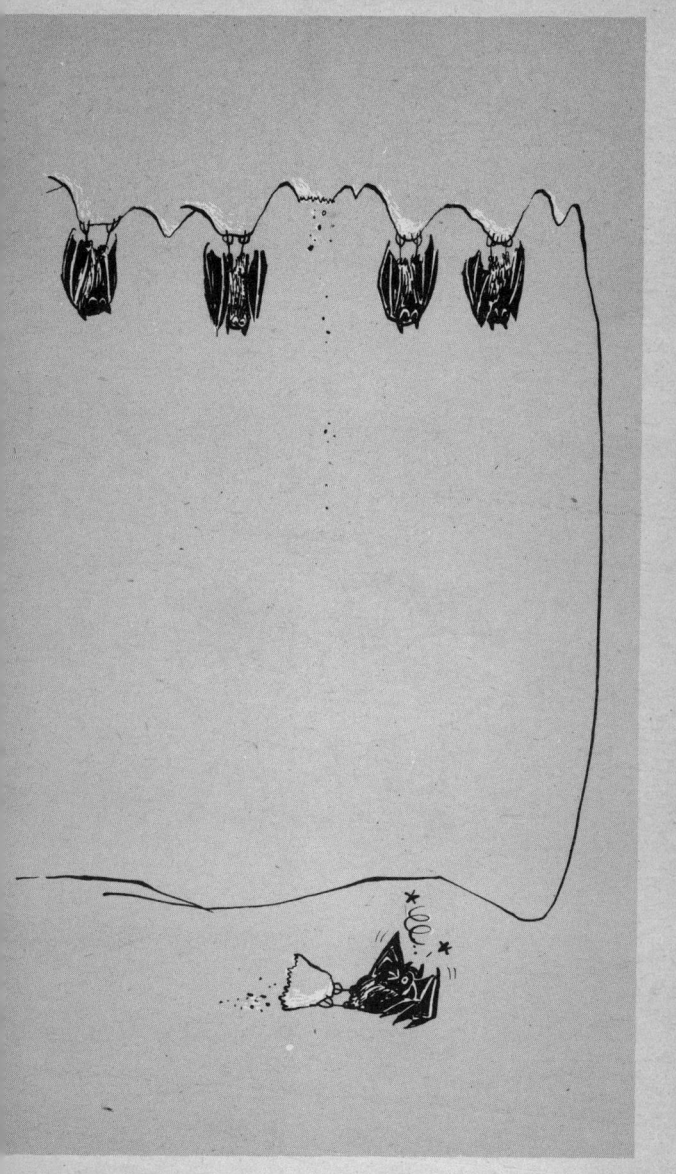

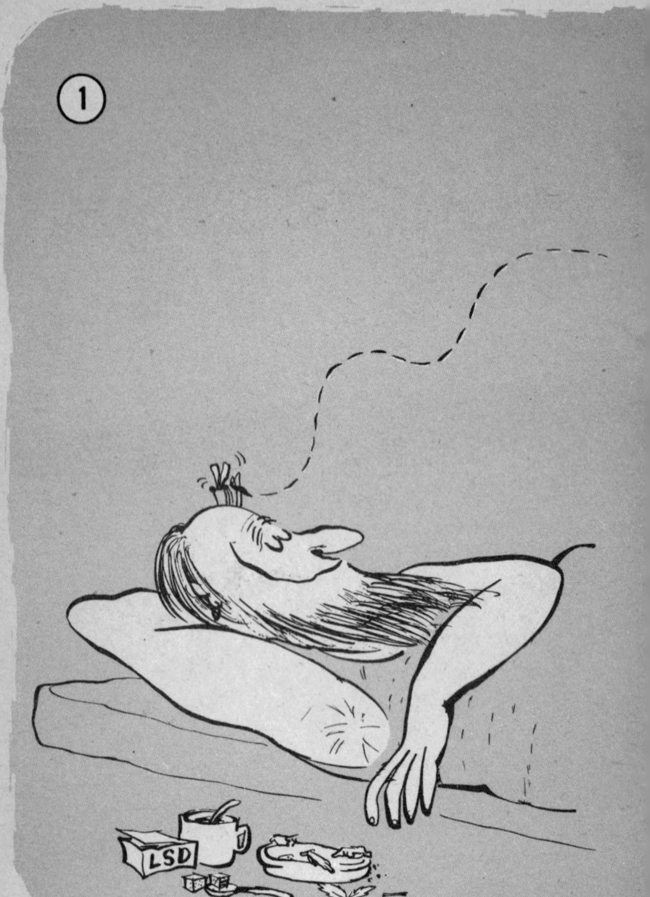
1
LSD

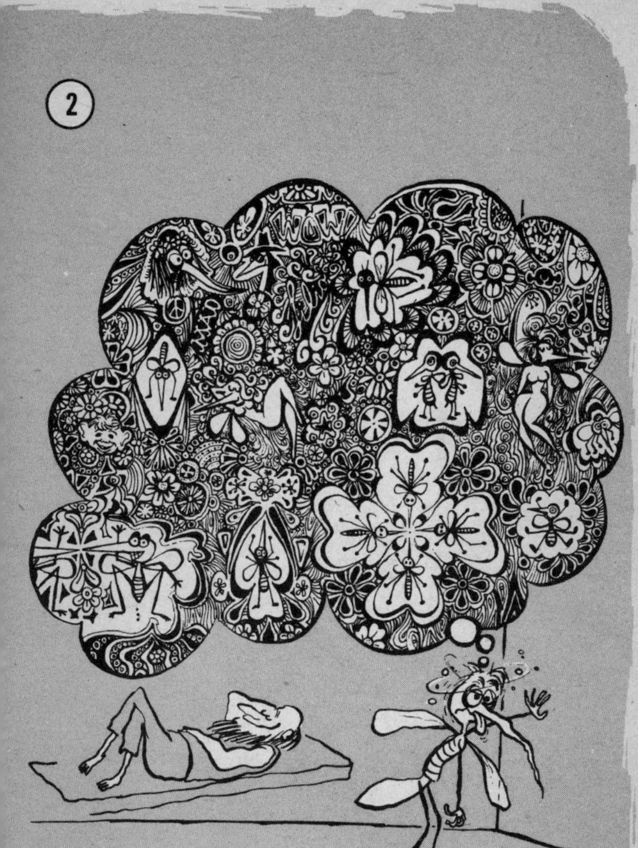
2
WOW
MAD

①

(2)

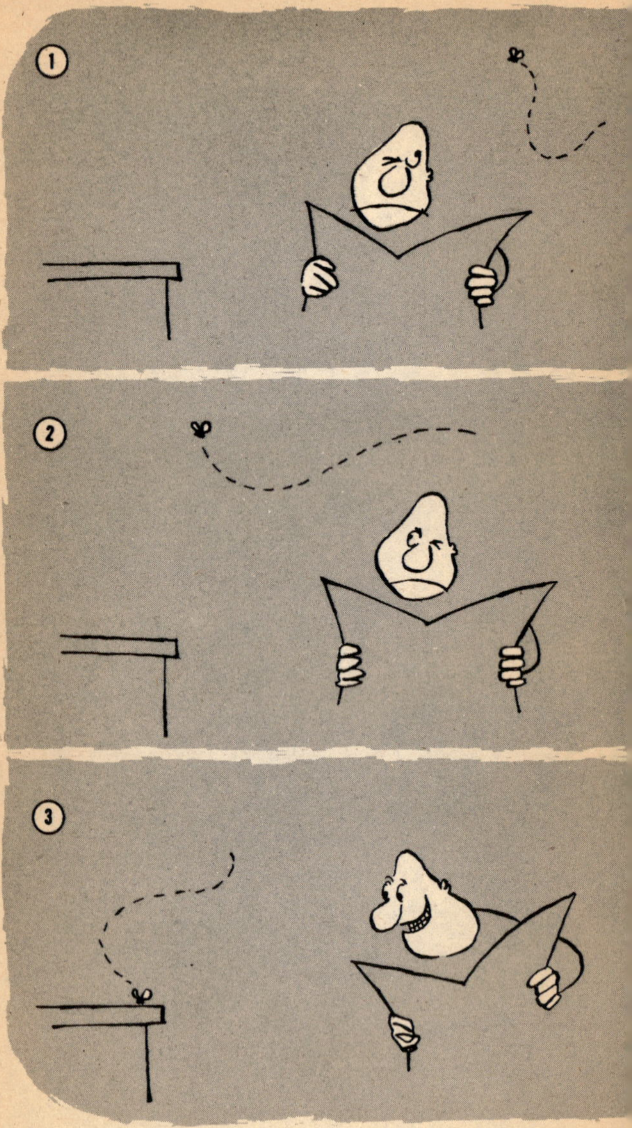
1
2
3

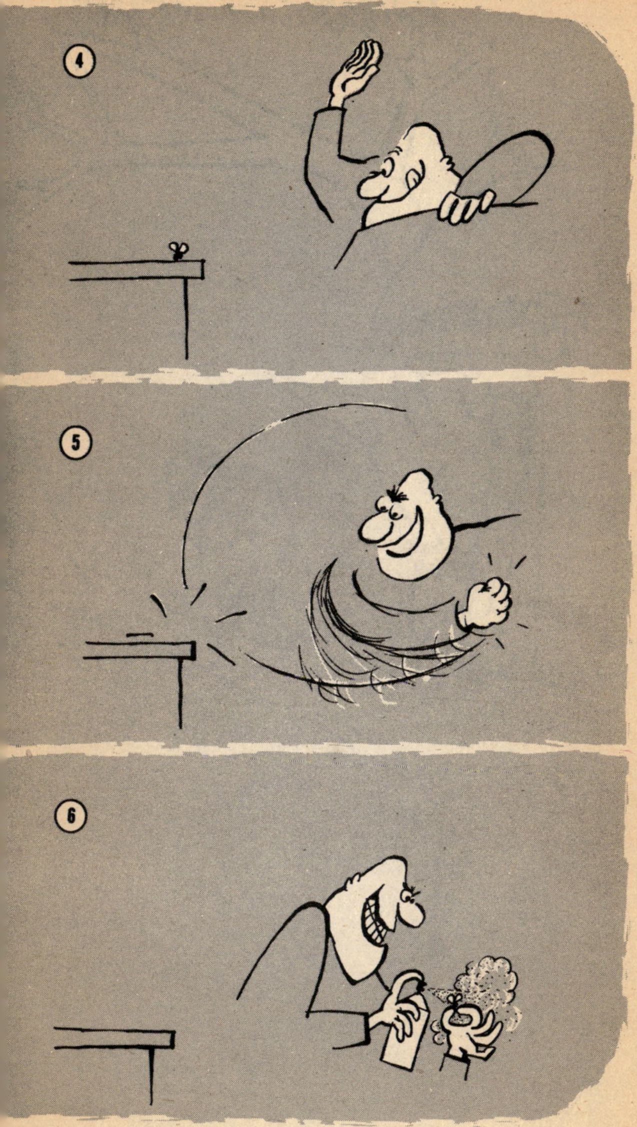
4
5
6

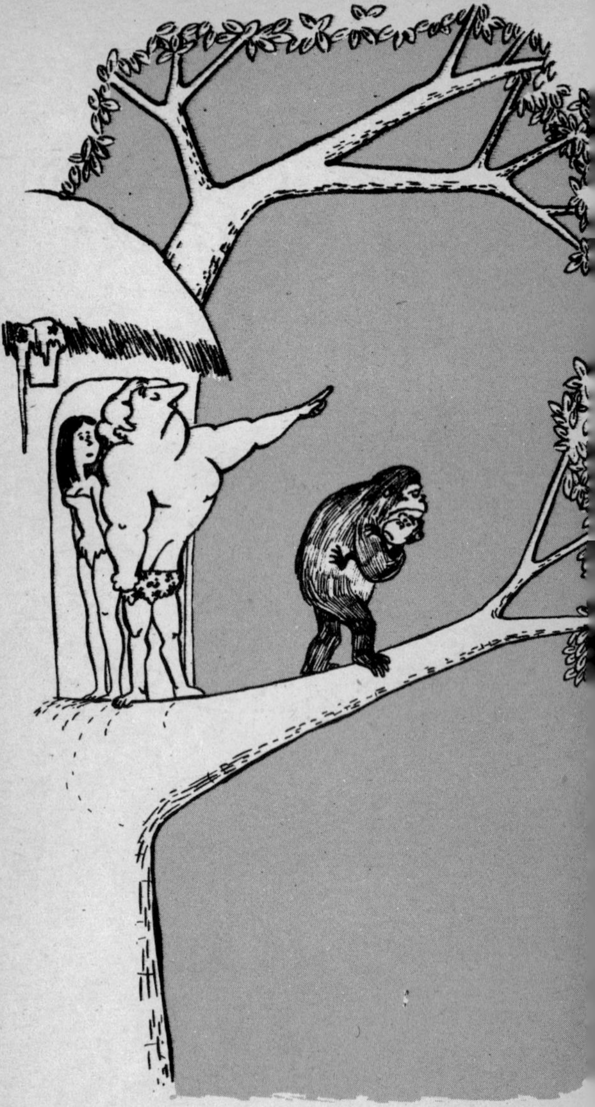

VIVA SUMMER!

ZZZ

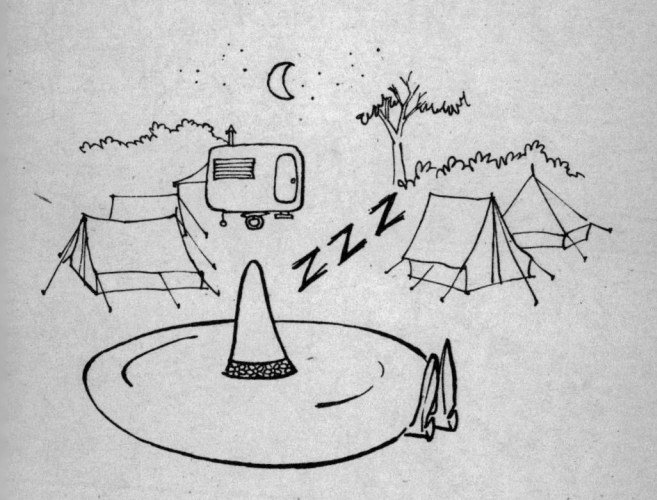

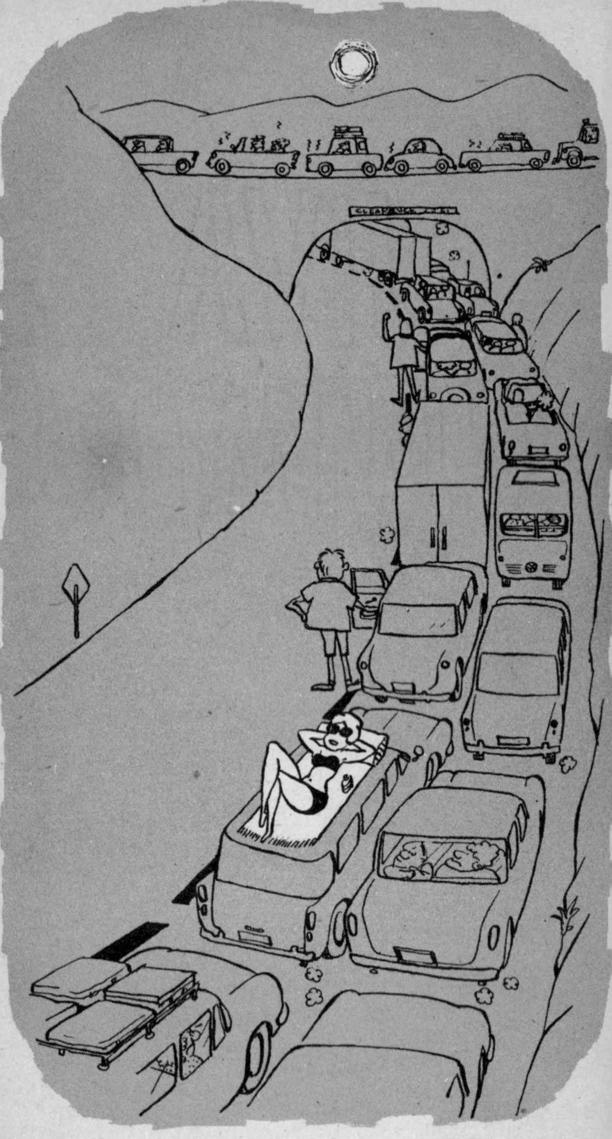

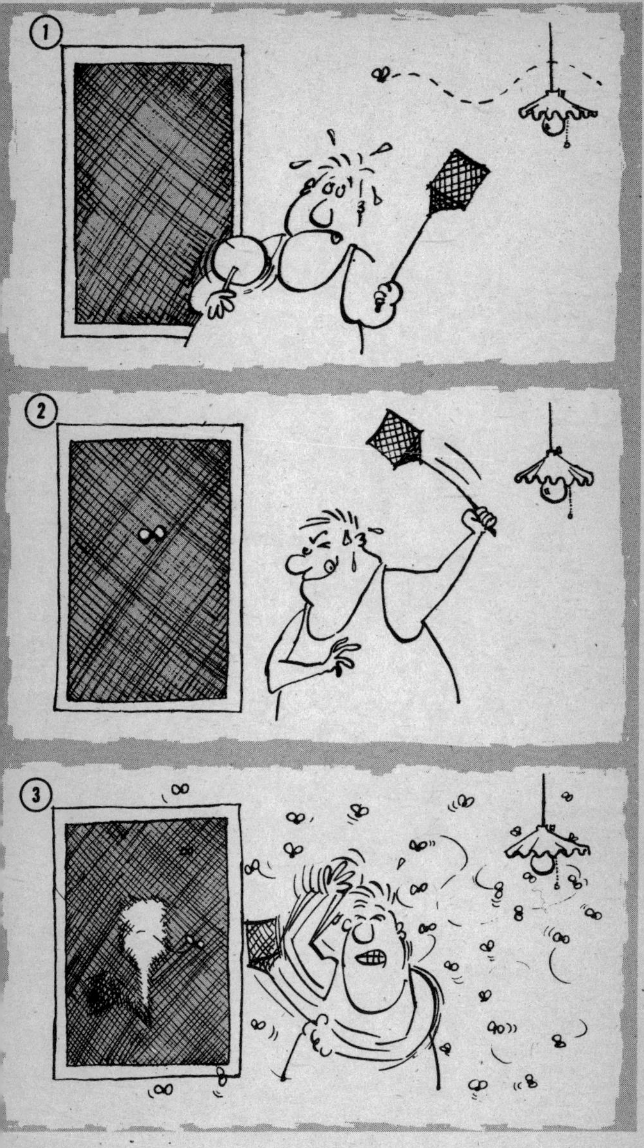

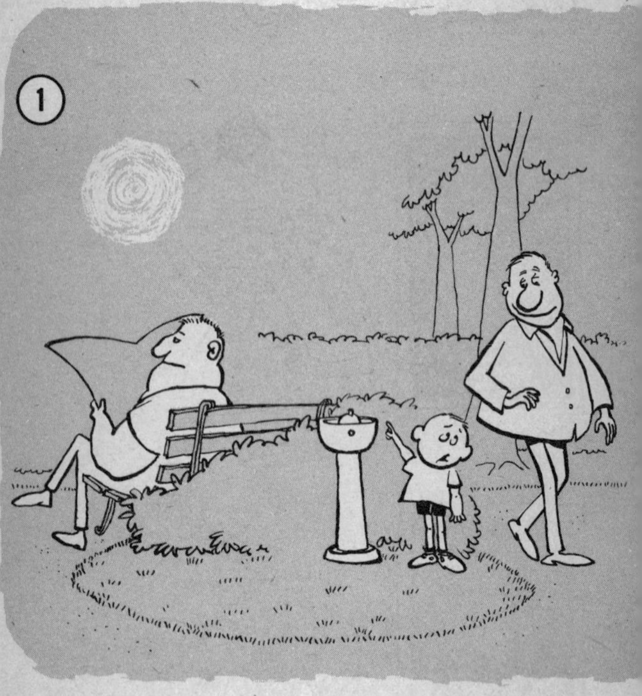
1

②

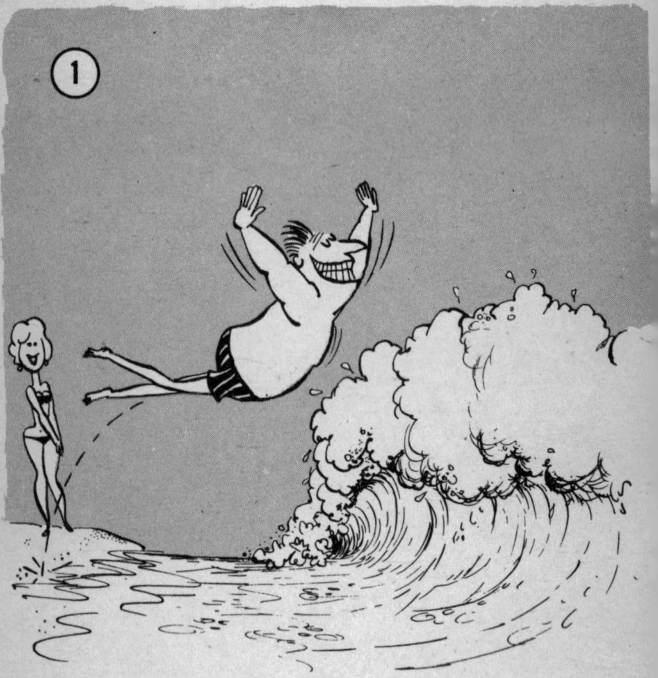
1

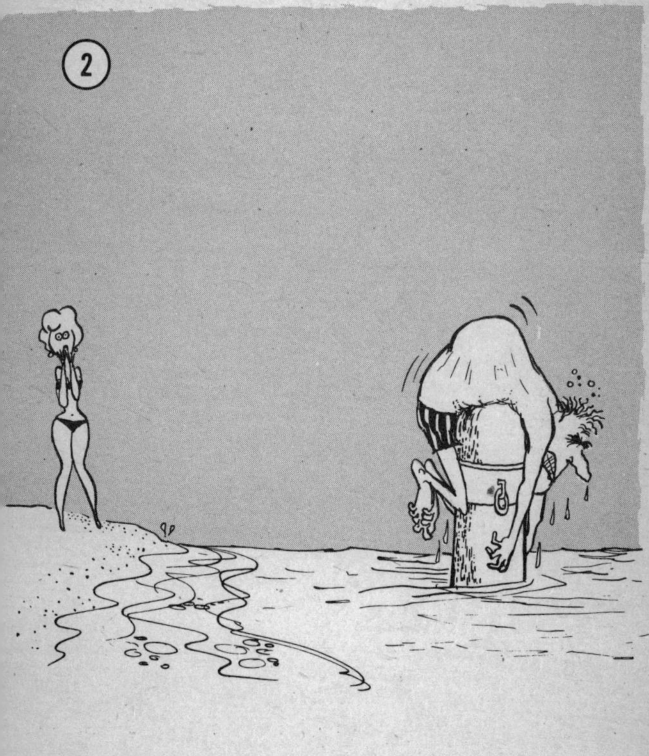
2

1

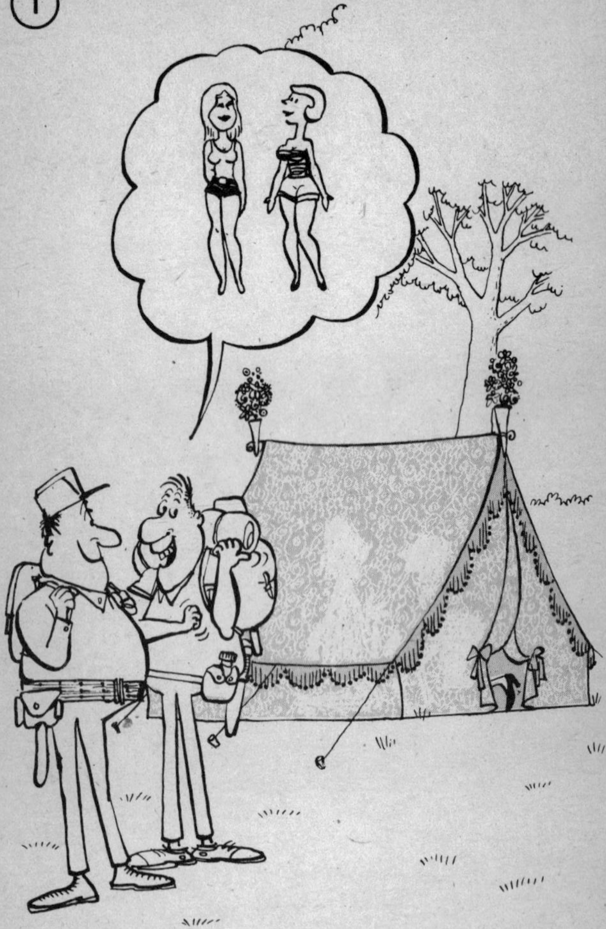

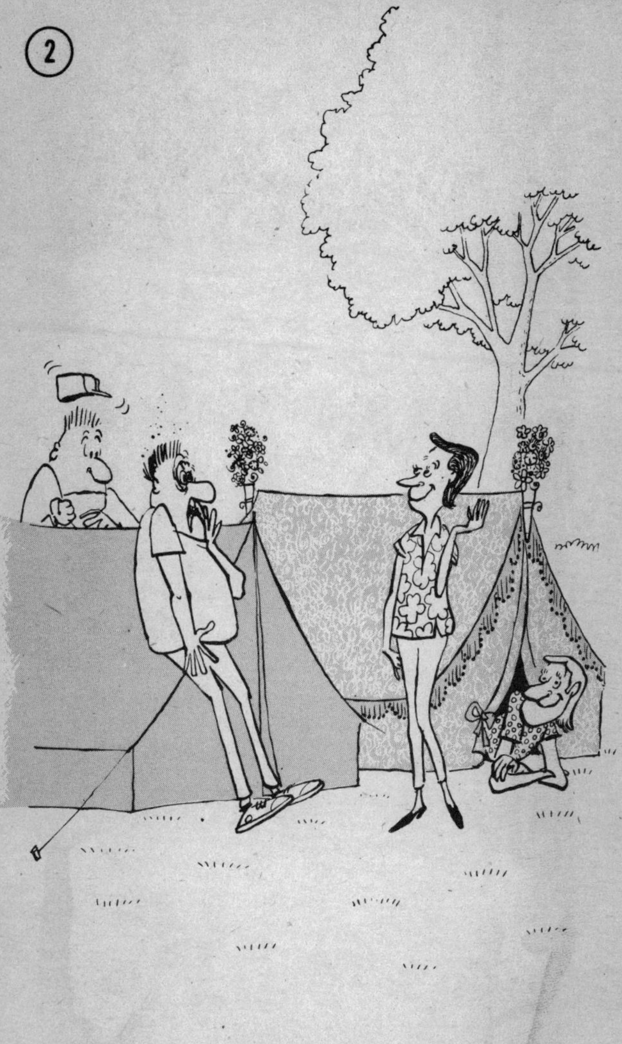

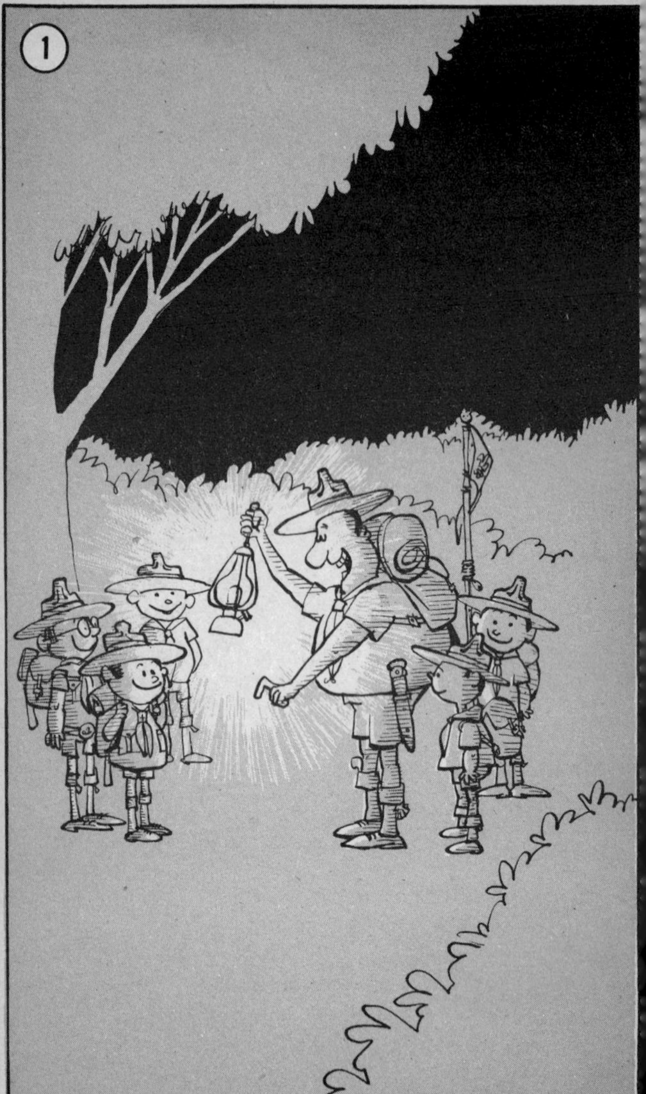

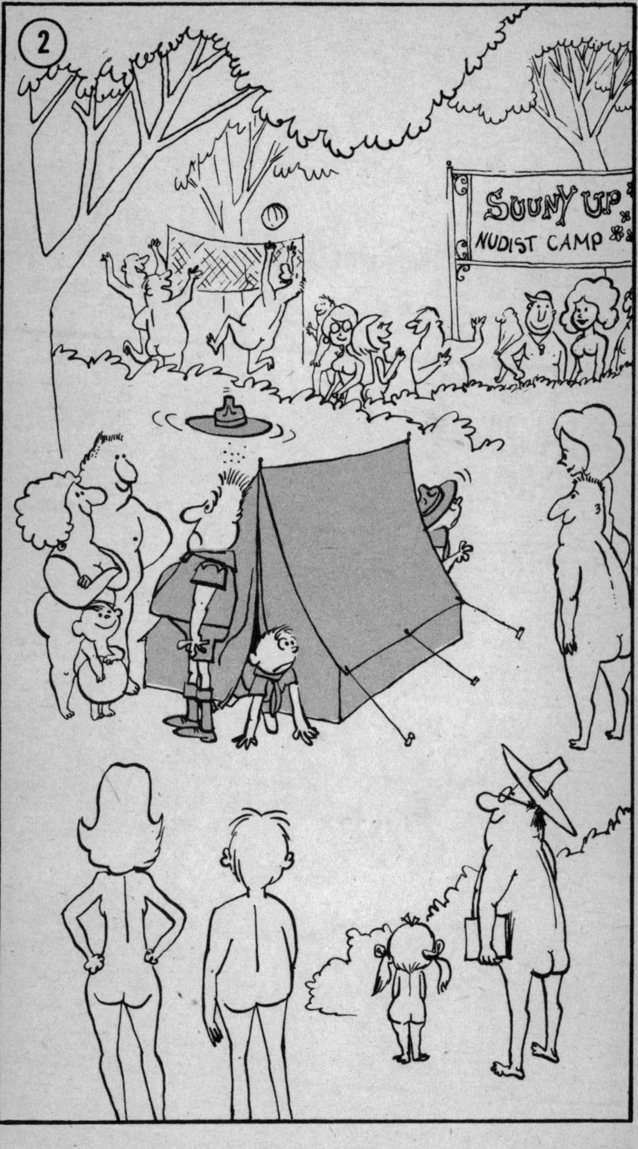
2
SUNNY UP
NUDIST CAMP

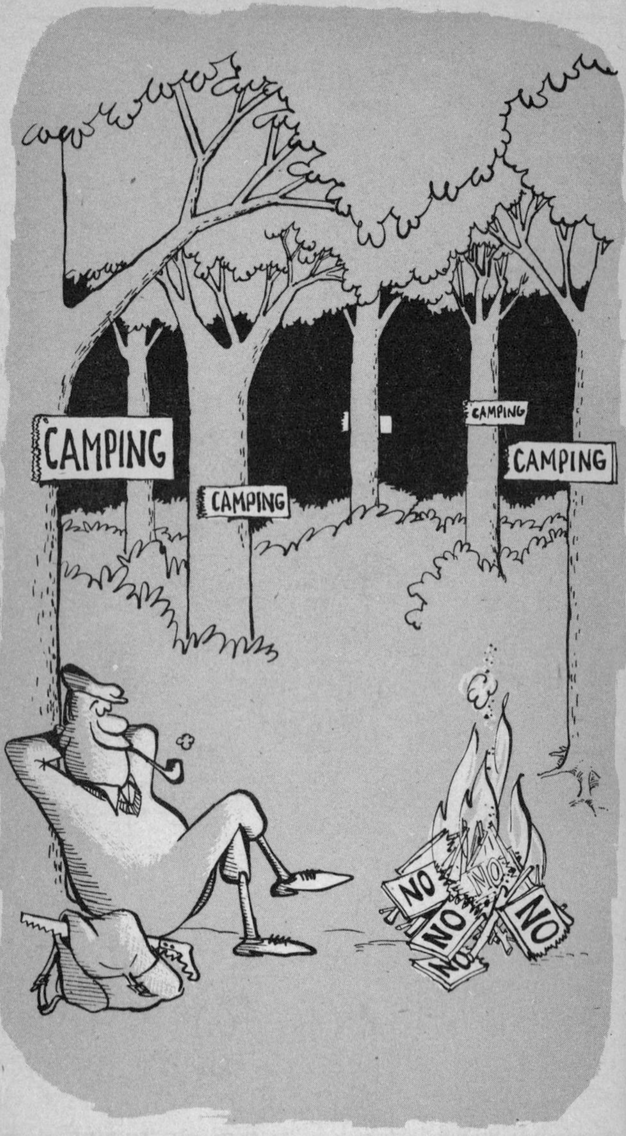
CAMPING
CAMPING
CAMPING
CAMPING
NO
NO
NO
NO
NO

VIVA REVOLUTIONS!

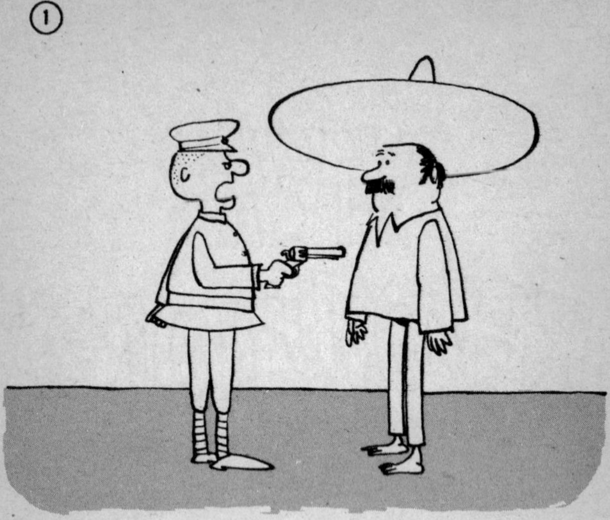

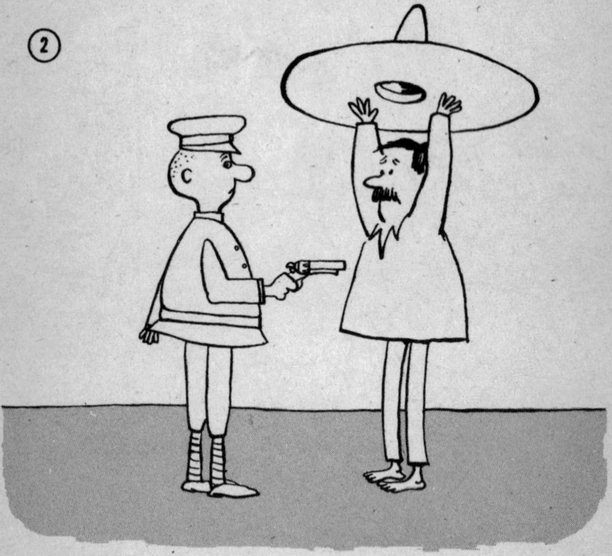

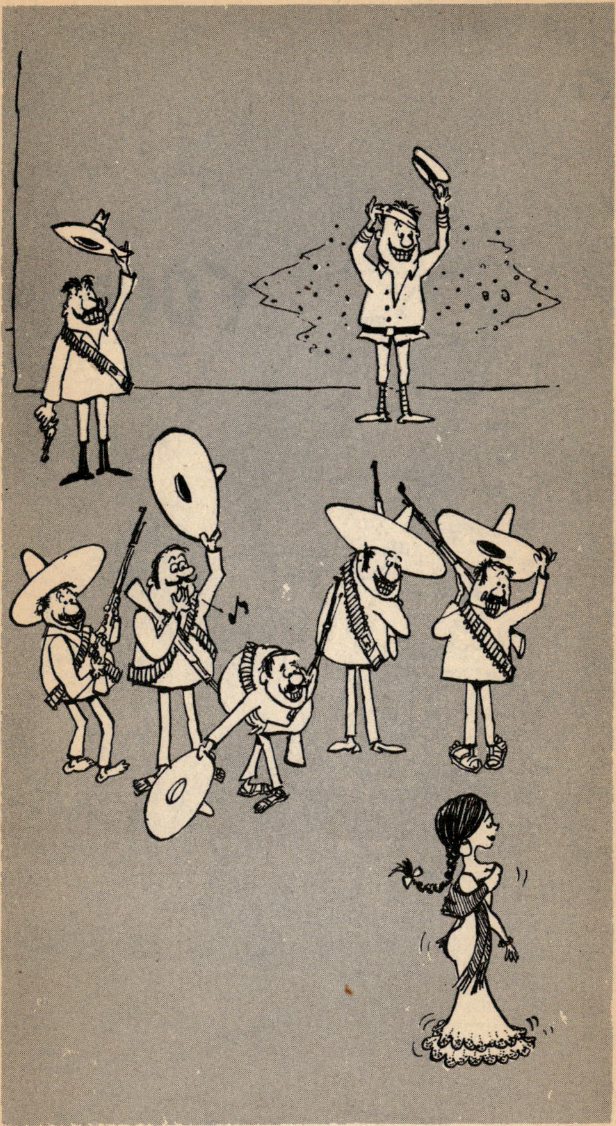

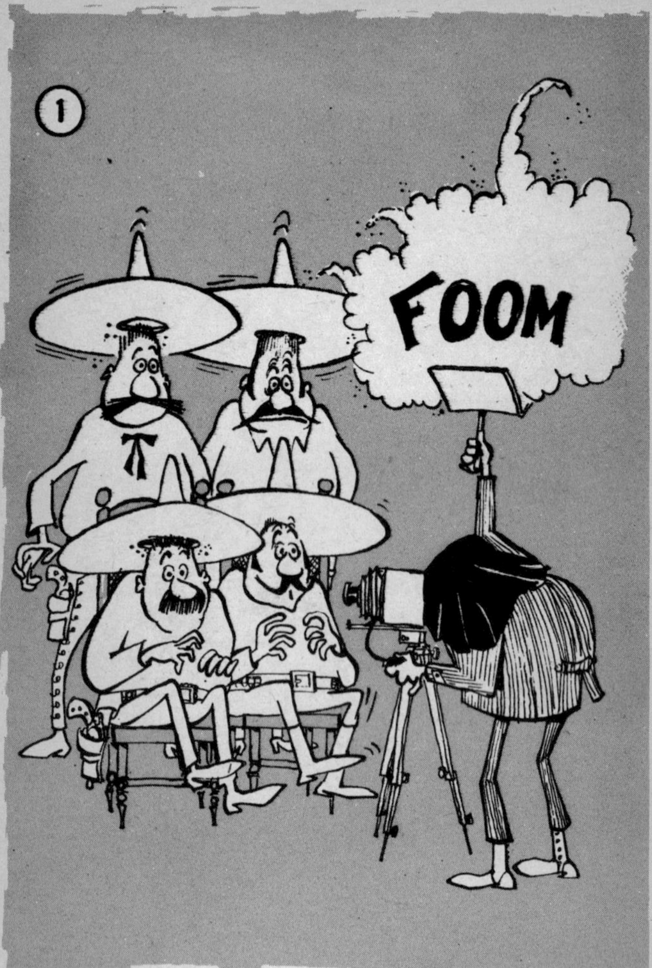
1
FOOM

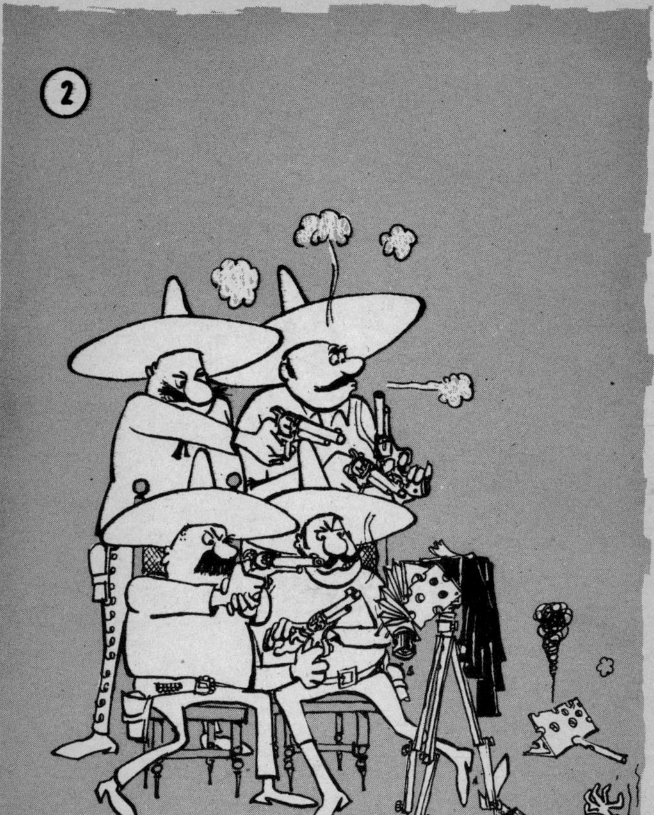
2

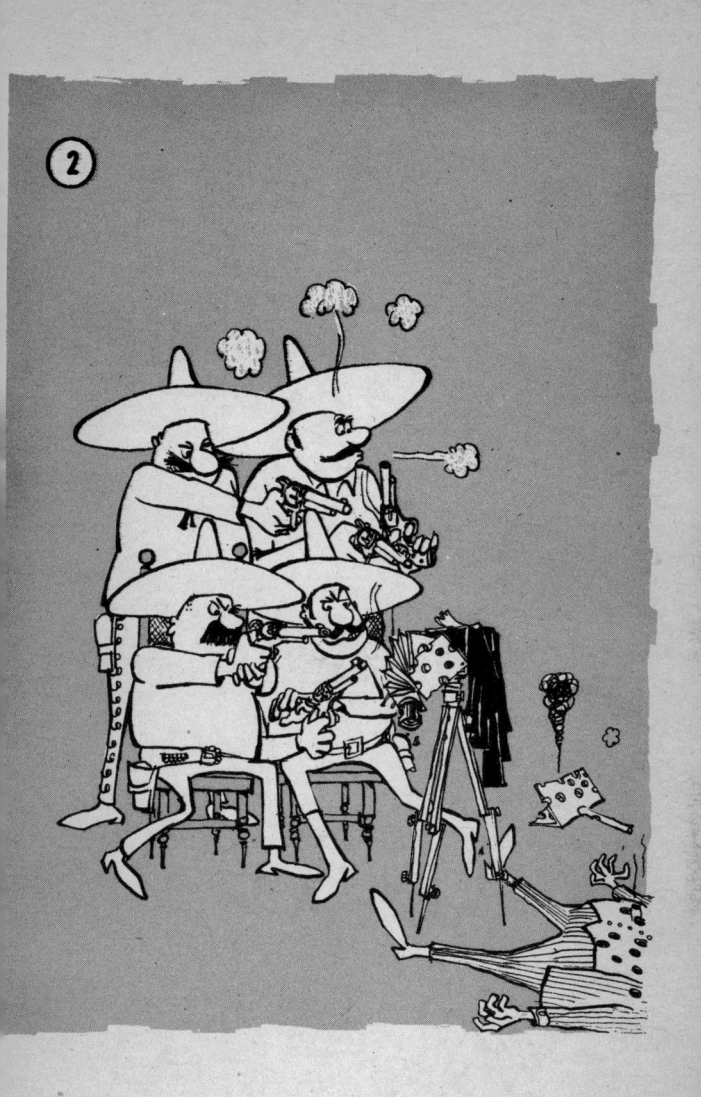

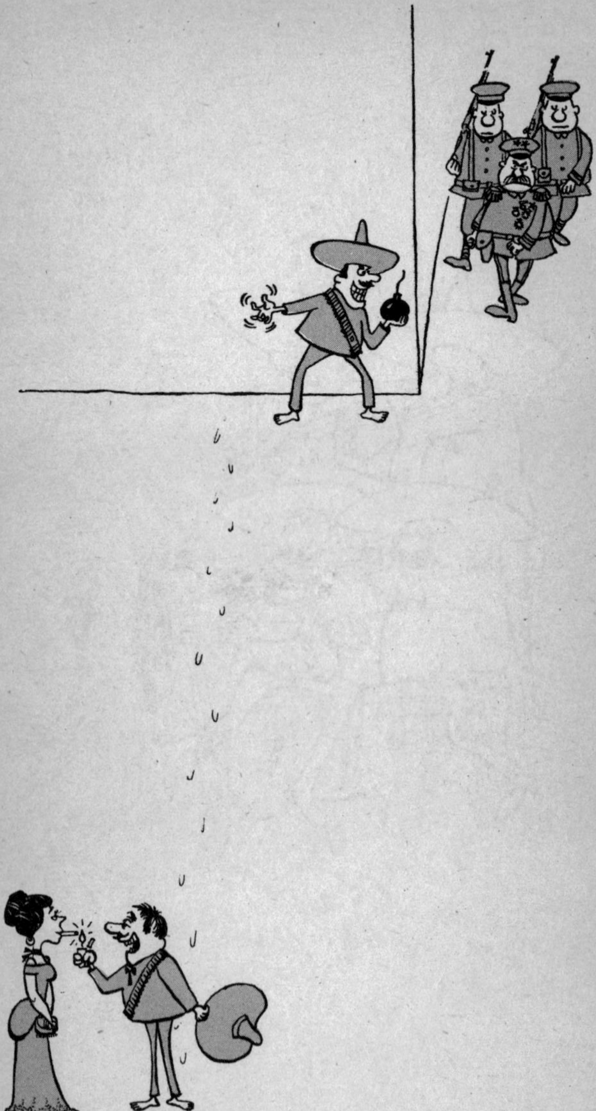

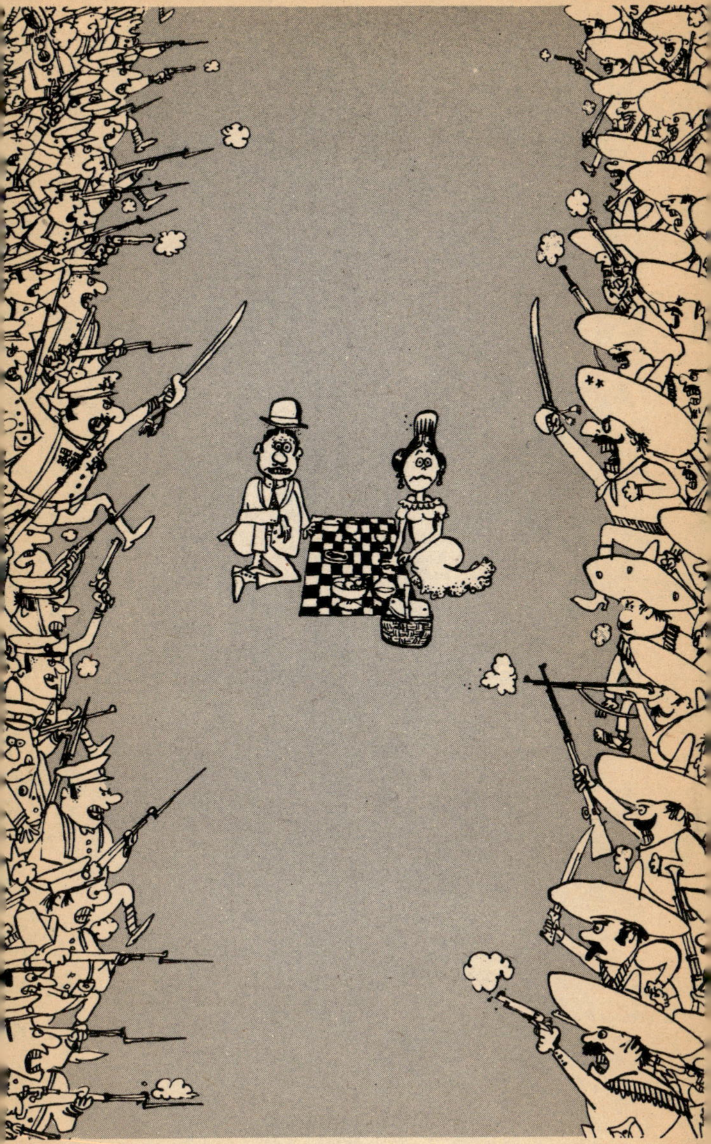

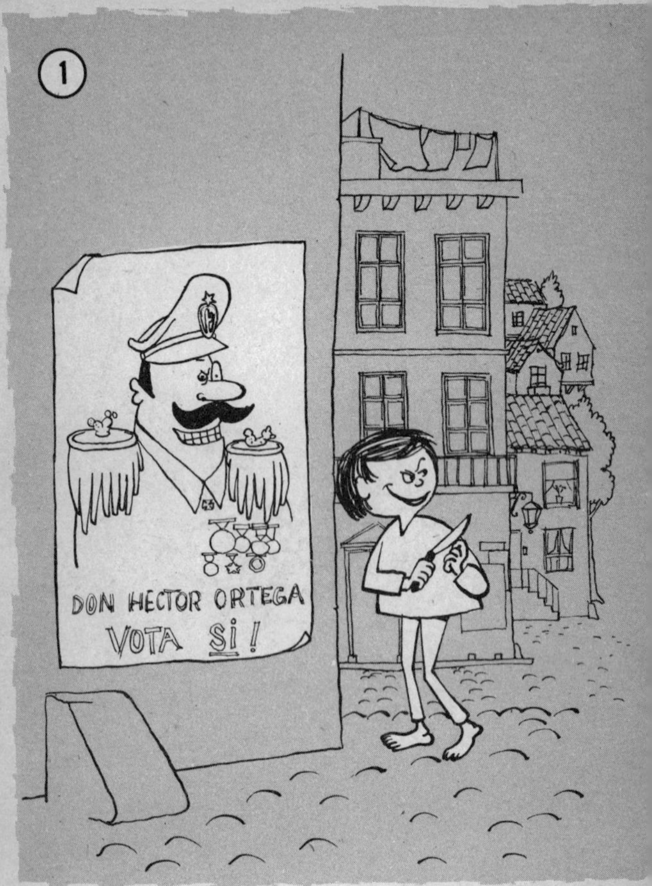
1
DON HECTOR ORTEGA
VOTA SI!

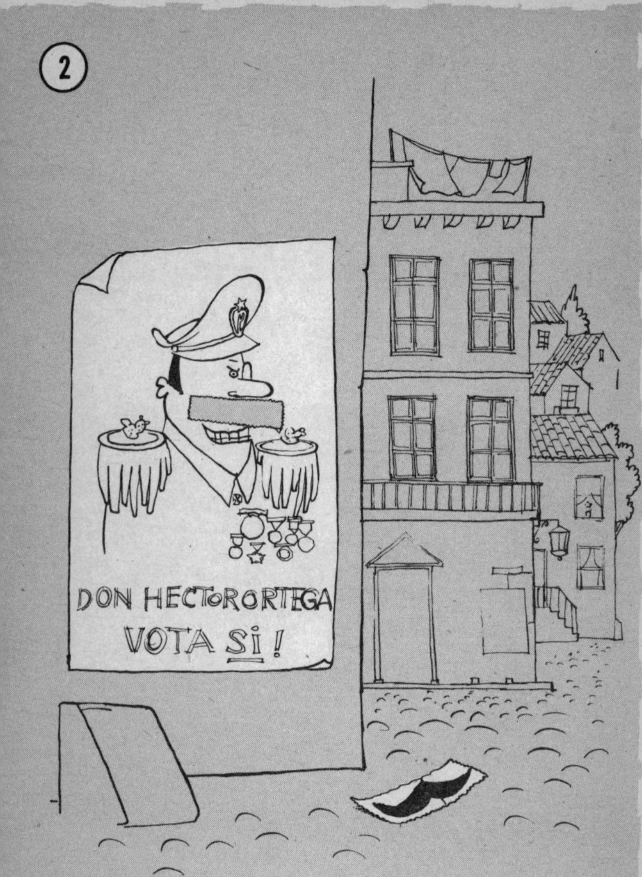
2
DON HECTORORTEGA
VOTA SI!

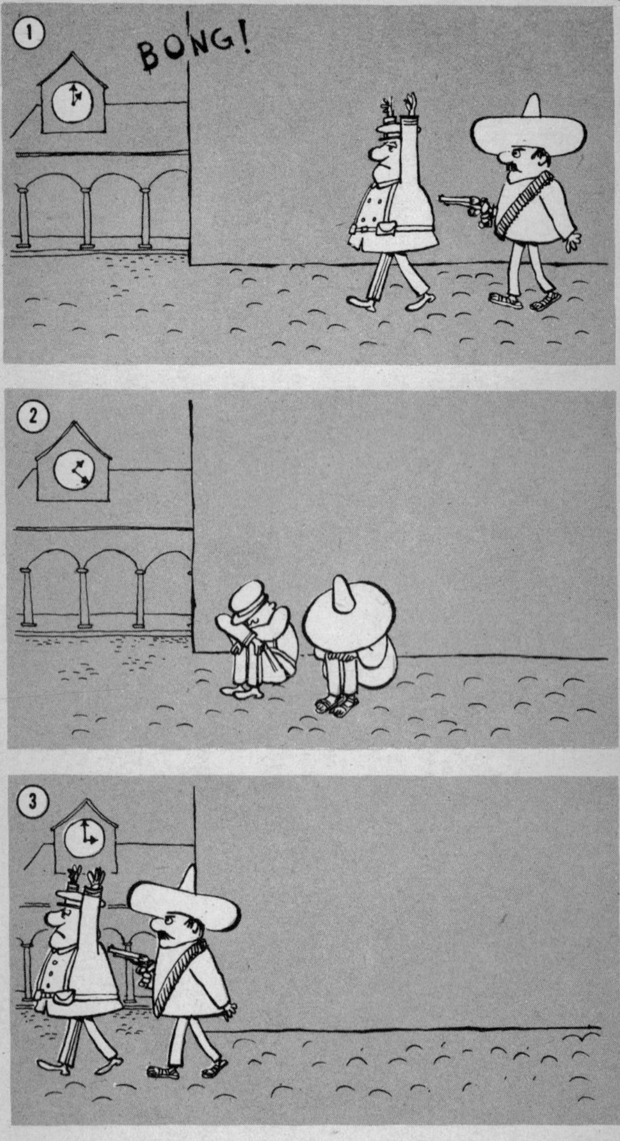
1
BONG!
2
3

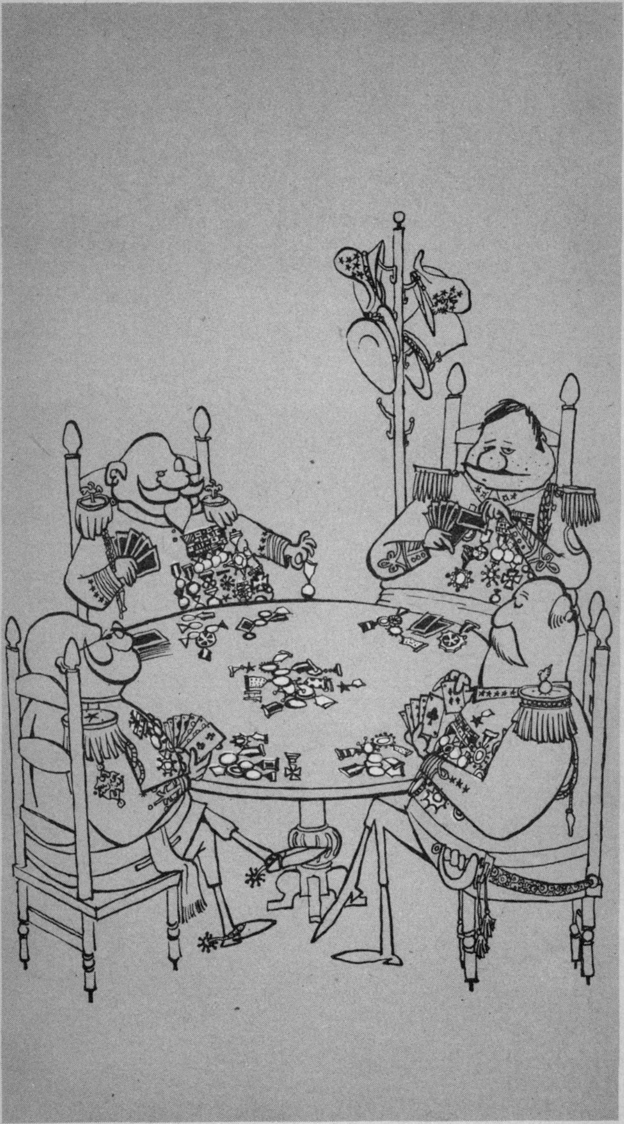

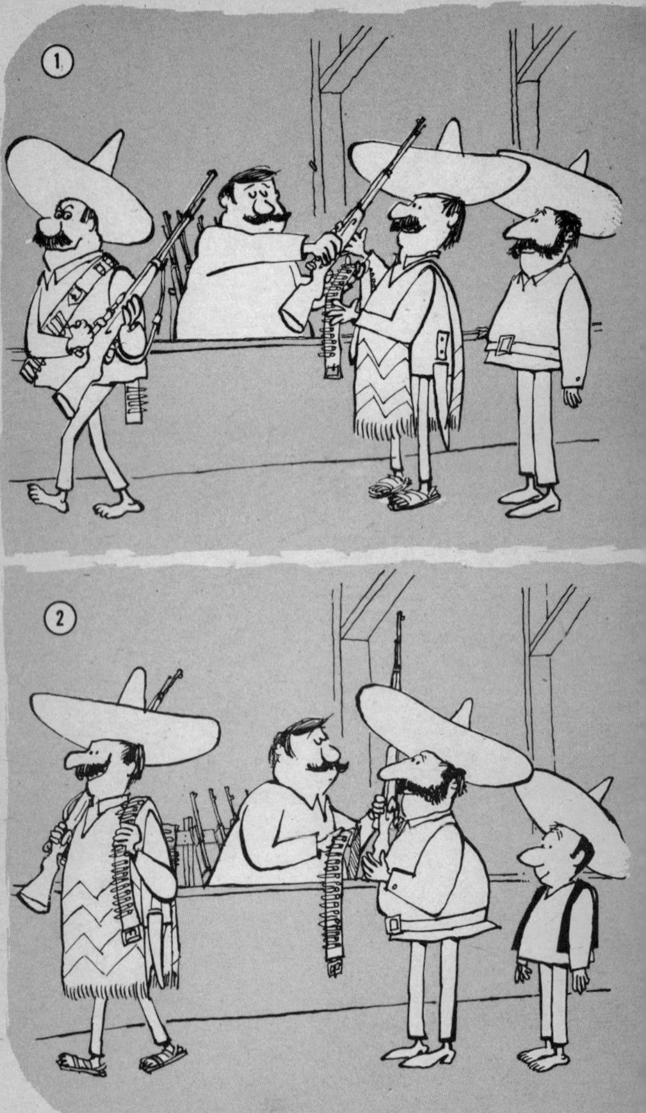

1
2

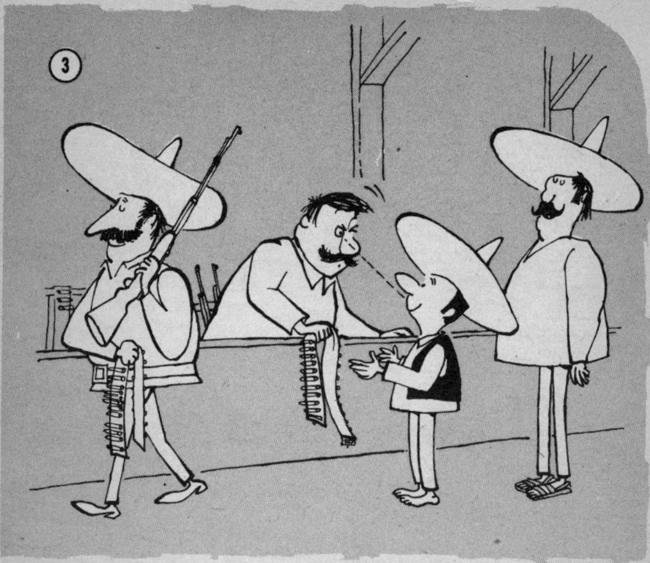

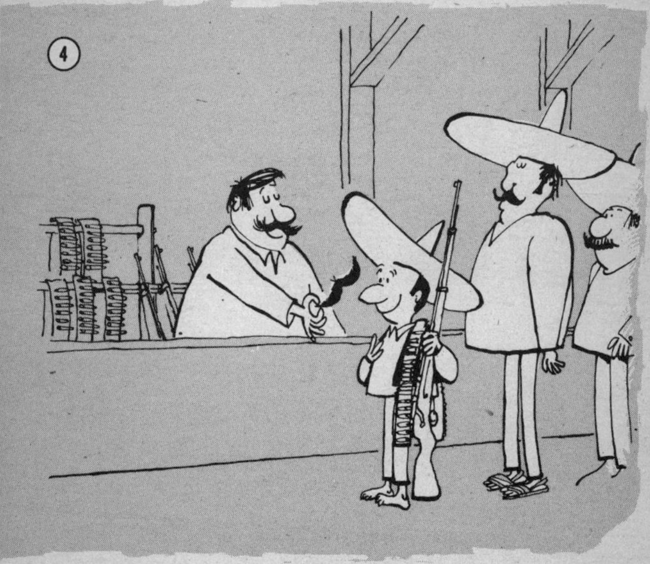

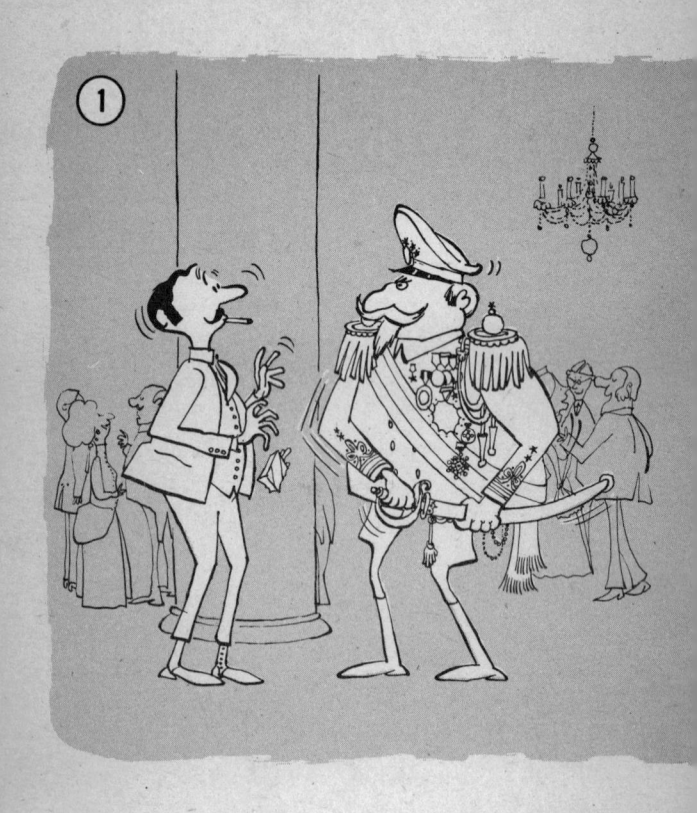
1

②

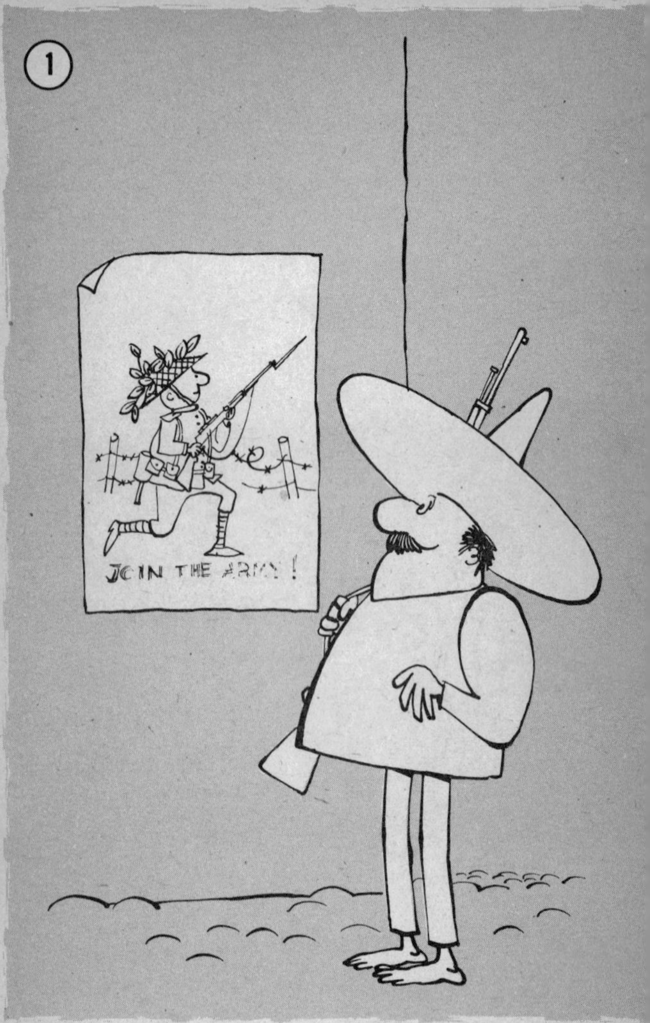
1
JOIN THE ARMY!

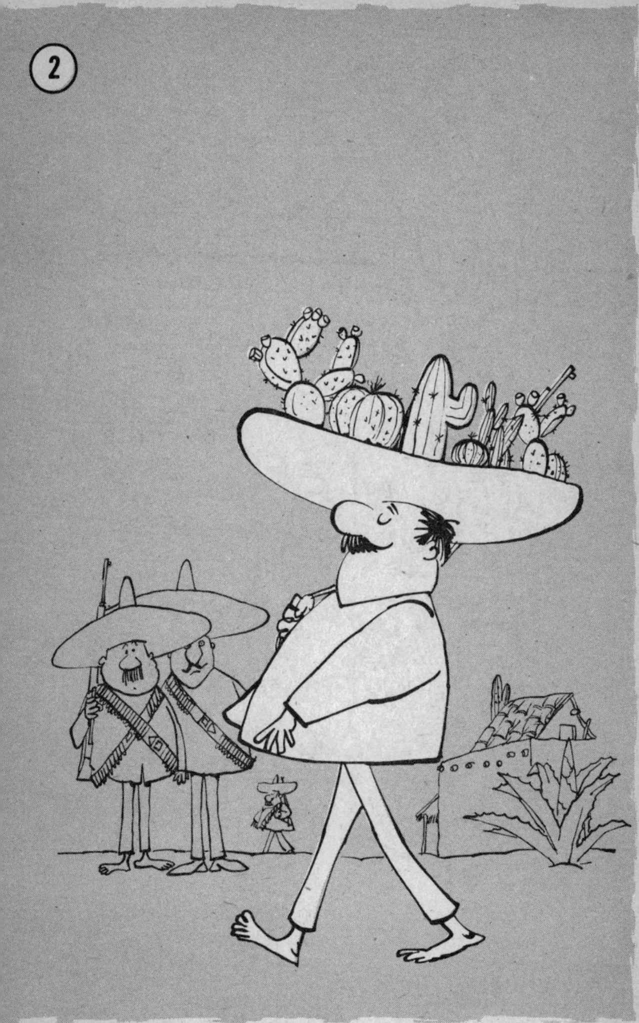
2

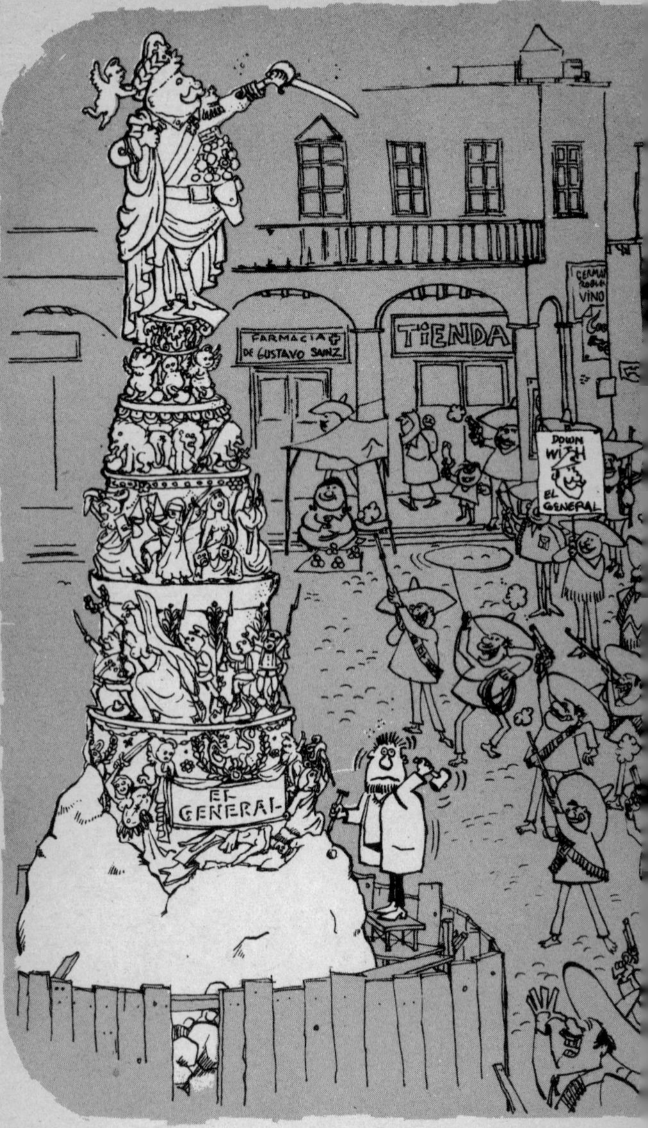
FARMACIA DE GUSTAVO SAINZ
TIENDA
VINO
DOWN WITH EL GENERAL
EL GENERAL

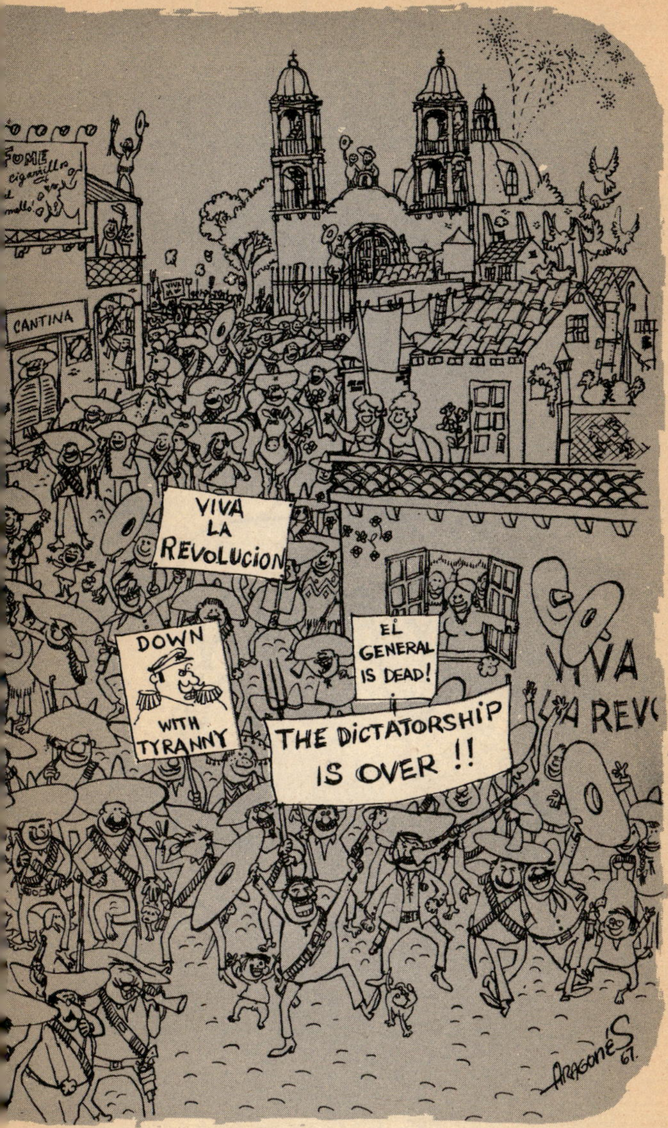
FUME
cigarrillos
CANTINA
VIVA
LA
REVOLUCION
DOWN
WITH
TYRANNY
EL
GENERAL
IS DEAD!
THE DICTATORSHIP
IS OVER !!
VIVA
LA REV
ARAGONÉS
67.

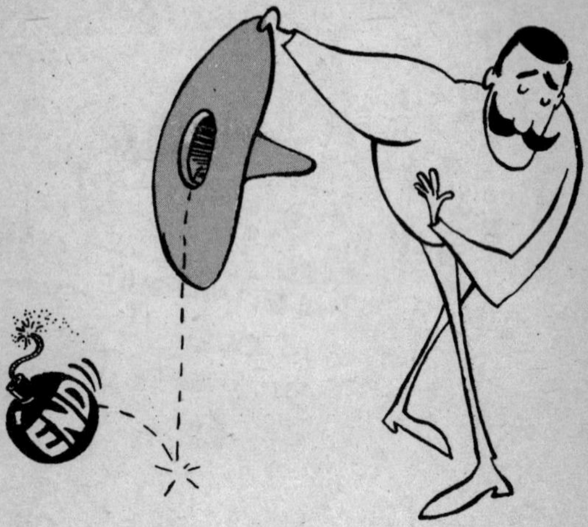
END